Watching and Waiting

Advent and Christmas Day by Day

R.E. Hasselbach

For my niece, Donna McNamara, M.D.,
and my nephew, Thomas Trauth.
I'm so proud of you, and I love you both!

Contents

Introduction

We have become so accustomed to the status quo that many of us have forgotten Christians are called to hope in the promises of the Lord. Jesus came and walked among us, the new Adam, to show us the full potential of our humanity. Each of us is born to bear the image of the God who created us. Sin and evil tarnished that image, but in Jesus, we see a sinless, obedient man who bears God's presence and power in His person. He is the one who atoned for all the brokenness and sin; He brought the redemption that only He could bring. On His cross, He carried our burdens. He suffered for us, faithful to the Father's justice and embodying the Father's love. Death couldn't hold Him, and in rising, He revealed the victory, once and for all, of life over death. God's victory was won. He sent the church His Spirit to be with us until the end of the ages. He instructed His disciples to bring the Good News of the victory to the ends of the earth, making disciples of "all nations, baptizing them in the name of the Father and of the Son, and of the Holy Spirit" (Matt. 28:19).

He promised that, as He came once as a child in Bethlehem, He will come again, in glory, to complete the work begun in the incarnation. This is the moment we eagerly anticipate. He will establish "a new heaven and a new earth" (Rev. 21:1) when He returns. In that glorious moment, God's kingdom will be fully realized, every tear will be wiped from every face, the brokenhearted will be made whole, the poor will be blessed with God's abundance, and Satan will be finally defeated. This is the hope that fills our hearts as we wait.

What do we do in the meantime as we wait for the end time? How should we wait for the return of the One who comes? The Gospels are clear: be alert, watchful, and on guard. We will never see Him coming if we don't know what we're looking for, and since we "do not know the day or the hour" (Matt. 25:13) we must always be ready and watchful. There is something wondrous about that watchfulness to which the Lord calls us: we may not see Him coming in glory every day, but we can see His presence in the face of a child, in the joy of a loved one, in the stranger we help, in our sick and suffering neighbors whom we visit, and in the grieving, as we share in their sorrow through our loving concern and give them the hope of our faith. Death has been defeated, and their loved ones are in the arms of the Great Lover who wills that none of His little ones be lost.

The end we wait for, though, will come. It will surprise even the ones who wait most diligently. It will be sudden, the Lord says, "like a thief in the night" (1 Thess. 5:2). When he comes, he will "make all things new" (Rev. 21:5)! Everything and everyone will be restored, and the dead will rise, even as the Lord did, to stand before Him and be judged by our just and loving Christ. The timing of this return is the Father's—not even Jesus could tell us when or even how this great, glorious, and dreadful Day of the Lord will occur. All we can say is that it will occur, and we must be prepared. This is why we must always be ready, living each day in readiness for His return.

In John's Revelation, we glimpse heaven preparing for the great rescue mission, which is the end time. John's vision was of God's throne room, where the Father sits in majesty, holding a scroll with writing on it and sealed with seven seals. The scroll contained the plans for God's final battle with evil, for the ultimate defeat of Satan and his collaborators. The seals kept the plan from being operational until someone worthy of opening the seals could be found, and no one in Heaven or on Earth or under the Earth could be found who was worthy to unseal and open the scroll.

All seemed lost to John, and he wept, but an elder came to him and said, "Do not weep! See, the Lion of the tribe of Judah, the Root of David, has triumphed. He is able to open the scroll and its seven seals" (Rev. 5:5). Who is the Lion of Judah, the one who triumphed? It is the Christ, Jesus. However, the vision gets more complex. John writes:

"Then I saw the Lamb, looking as if it had been slain, standing at the center of the throne, encircled by the four living creatures and the elders… He went and took the scroll from the right hand of the one who sat on the throne, and when he had taken it, the four living creatures and the twenty-four elders fell down before the Lamb" (Rev. 5:6-7).

The Lion and the Lamb are one. The power of God is one with the meekness of the Lamb. The victory of the Lion was won on Calvary. It is the cross, which Paul calls the "power of God and the wisdom of God" (1 Cor. 24). Jesus' obedience, literally his sacrifice is what makes Him, and Him alone, worthy to take the scroll, break open its seals, and begin the final victory of good over evil, life over death. This unity of the Lion and the Lamb is a testament to the strength and security we find in our faith.

As we watch and wait, this is for whom we wait and who is coming: no one less than the crucified and risen One. He brings us life, light, and restoration of all we love and have ever loved. We are waiting for the Lion of Judah, who is the Lamb of God. He has carried our sins to the cross and washed them white as snow. The Lamb is our Good Shepherd who has walked with us through every dark valley; He is returning to lead us to the house of the Lord forever.

In this book, you will find a Scripture reading, a lesson, and an activity for each day of the Advent and Christmas seasons. I hope they will help you to watch and wait for the Lord throughout this holy time of the year.

\#

First Sunday of Advent

Scripture

"Be on guard! Be alert! You do not know when that time will come. It's like a man going away: He leaves his house and puts his servants in charge, each with their assigned task, and tells the one at the door to keep watch. Therefore keep watch because you do not know when the owner of the house will come back—whether in the evening, or at midnight, or when the rooster crows, or at dawn. If he comes suddenly, do not let him find you sleeping. What I say to you, I say to everyone: 'Watch!'" (Mark 13:33–37).

Reflection

Years ago, I drove Fran, a young friend of mine, to the airport to pick up her parents who were returning from a well-deserved vacation in Europe. They had been gone for what seemed to her a long time and she missed them terribly. While she was waiting at the airport, Fran stood on tiptoes looking above the heads of the assembled crowd to catch the first glimpse of her mom and dad as they came out of the airport security area and into view. She was filled with anticipation: this would be a joyful reunion. Other people in the same area, waiting to pick up other travelers, waited differently: some seemed bored, others looked tired, and many looked a little annoyed. The way we wait depends on what we are waiting for.

Christians wait for the promised return of Jesus. The One who came *will* come again. The early church lived in the expectation of the return in glory of the Crucified-and-Risen One. Over the years, as His return has been delayed (from our perspective) we have grown weary, we tend to forget we are called to be alert, watchful, and prepared for the day of His coming.

On the night before He died, Jesus assured His closest friends that, while He was about to leave them, He would return to them. Knowing how much they would miss Him he told them:

"Do not let your hearts be troubled. You believe in God; believe also in me. My Father's house has many rooms; if that were not so, would I have told you that I am going there to prepare a place for you? And if I go and prepare a place for you, I will come back and take you to be with me that you also may be where I am. You know the way to the place where I am going"(John 15:1-4).

We are waiting for Jesus' return to bring His saving work to completion and to take His beloved people home! We are waiting for the vindication of Jesus and of our faith in Jesus as our Lord and Savior. We are waiting for the end of history. We are waiting for the victory of our God and of His Christ.

As Jesus ascended having finished his earthly mission His disciples watched as He disappeared from their sight. As they gazed upward, two angels appeared to them with a warning: "Men of Galilee,' they said, 'why do you stand here looking into the sky? This same Jesus, who has been taken from you into heaven, will come back in the same way you have seen him go into heaven" (Acts 1: 10–11). The angels' message, distilled to its basic meaning was "Don't just stand there; get to work! Do something."

The angels reminded those disciples, *and us*, that there is an appropriate way to wait. Peter tells us as much in his first letter: "The end of all things is near. Therefore be alert and of sober mind so that you may pray" (1 Peter 4:7).

Jesus, in the gospel, tells us while we are waiting, we don't know *when* He will arrive, but whenever it is, He will be unexpected. He could catch us off guard and asleep unless we take His warning to heart.

Until He returns, He has put us, His servants, in charge of His mission to the world. We, like the Lord himself, must bring the good news to the end of the earth: to the poor, we are to bring the message of God's abundant love, to the blind, we are to bring sight that comes from the Light of the World, to the broken, we are to bring healing, to those in bondage, we are to bring liberation. We are the heralds of the Great King. The mission requires us to use both our voice and our choices. We are to share the power of Christ and of faith in Him with the people we meet. Every Christian has a unique story—it is the story of how God, in Christ, has moved in our lives. Some of those stories are dramatic, others quite ordinary, but all show some aspect of the power of God to transform our lives.

Our words are not enough. We must follow them up with lives lived well. Peter writes:

"Therefore, with minds that are alert and fully sober, set your hope on the Grace to be brought to you when Jesus Christ is revealed at his coming… do not conform to the evil desires you had when you lived in ignorance, but just as he who called you is holy, so be holy in all you do; for it is written: 'Be holy because I am holy'" (1 Peter 1:13–16).

There is nothing more important than fulfilling our mission as we wait in joyful hope of the Lord's return. We are to continue to make him known to the world—with both our lips and our lives—and bring His salvation to the ends of the earth, starting right where we are now.

Activity
Pray for the grace of deep conversion, and for the wisdom to know when, where, and how to share the Lord's good news as it has manifested in your life.

Prayer
God, our Father, you created the world and everything in it, making humans in your likeness

to bear your image. You love everything You created, and when we sinned, You did not stop loving us.

#

Notes

5

Monday of the First Week of Advent

Scripture
"All of us have become like one who is unclean,
    and all our righteous acts are like filthy rags;
we all shrivel up like a leaf,
    and like the wind, our sins sweep us away.
No one calls on your name
    or strives to lay hold of you;
for you have hidden your face from us
    and have given us over to our sins.
Yet you, Lord, are our Father.
    We are the clay, you are the potter;
    we are all the work of your hand.
Do not be angry beyond measure, Lord;
    do not remember our sins forever.
Oh, look on us, we pray,
    for we are all your people.
After all this, Lord, will you hold yourself back?
    Will you keep silent and punish us beyond measure?"
    (Isaiah 64:6–8, 12).

Reflection
Advent invites us to know who we really are.

The humility of the human condition is captured beautifully by Isaiah: "All of us have become like one who is unclean, and all our righteous acts are like filthy rags." It can't be plainer than that. We are nothing as we stand before God, and we are powerless to do anything to improve our standing or to save ourselves. Our best efforts (our righteousness) are nothing but filth before the One who is holy. But Isaiah does not leave us utterly hopeless, rather, he calls upon the Lord, begging for mercy and for another chance.

God is also our Father; He is the Creator, and we are His creation. Just as a potter can rework his clay when an artifact isn't turning out just right, so can God reshape us, reform us, and redeem us, for we are the work of His hand.

There is an ancient bit of rabbinic wisdom that captures the paradox we find in Isaiah. It goes like this:

A man should always wear a garment with two pockets. In one pocket, there should be a note that reads, "I am but dust and ashes." In the other pocket, there should be another note that reads, "For me, the world was made."

We live within this paradox. We *are* but dust and ashes. Our lives are a mere flicker in the onward sweep of history. As the world judges importance, we are nothing, even the most important of us. Our lives are fleeting and brief. We leave little behind once they are over.

But for each of us, the world was made! Our lives are not random; we are not here at this time and in these circumstances by chance. We are creatures of a loving God who has revealed Himself to us as our Father. The psalmist writes:

"You created my inmost being;
    You knit me together
        in my mother's womb.
I praise you because I am fearfully
        and wonderfully made;
    Your works are wonderful,
    I know that full well" (Psalm 139:13–14).

Yes, we are but dust and ashes, but each of us is fearfully and wonderfully made, from the moment of our conception the Father is at work knitting us together in our mother's womb to be His child, His beloved, His image.

Our humanity was made to bear His image and likeness, and in the Christ, born in Bethlehem and coming again to set his people free at the culmination of history, we see the great dignity of our flesh and blood—it has been made to bear divinity, and in Jesus of Nazareth that is just what happened.

He reveals to us the possibility of our humanity to incarnate the presence of God.

Prayer
Father, we stand before you as dust and ashes, we are nothing before your majesty. Yet You have given us the right to be your adopted children through our faith in Your Son, Jesus. Deepen our faith in Him and allow us to express our faith in Him through our words and actions, today and always, as we await his return.

Activity
Take two index cards and write notes to yourself. On one write: I am but dust and ashes. And on the other write: For me, the world was made. Carry them with you, one in your left pocket and the other in your right, as reminders of both the humility and the profound dignity of your existence, an existence which is in itself, a gift from God.

#

Notes

Tuesday of the First Week of Advent

Scripture
"On this mountain, the Lord Almighty will prepare
a feast of rich food for all peoples,
a banquet of aged wine—
the best of meats and the finest of wines.
    On this mountain, he will destroy
the shroud that enfolds all peoples,
the sheet that covers all nations;
He will swallow up death forever.
The Sovereign Lord will wipe away the tears
from all faces;
He will remove His people's disgrace
from all the earth.
The Lord has spoken.
    In that day they will say,
    'Surely this is our God;
we trusted in Him, and He saved us.
This is the Lord, we trusted in him;
let us rejoice and be glad in his salvation'" (Isaiah 25:6–9).

Reflection
I read this passage from Isaiah recently at the funeral of a young woman. She was only fifty-three. It was a sad moment: her mother, from whom she was estranged, didn't come to mourn her daughter, and friends who should have been at the service chose not to come. The deceased woman, I'll call her Kate, made many mistakes. She was in the thrall of drugs, and substances that ended up killing her. Kate's stepmother, who arranged her funeral, told me that "if there was a mistake to make, Kate would make it: bad choices, bad friends, bad habits." But it wasn't always thus.

There was an array of pictures showing Kate as a beautiful child with sparkling eyes and so much potential. Her smile as a teenager was radiant, and I could see the joy in her long-ago face in a picture taken on a trip to the shore. There was such potential, but in the end, it was squandered, and Kate seemed to have ended her time on earth as a lost soul.

Israel, in the time of Isaiah, also appeared lost: it had betrayed its God, failing to live in His righteousness. It had broken its covenant with Him and disobeyed His law. In its dereliction, Israel neglected the poor, the marginalized, and the broken. God's holy people abandoned true worship and turned to worshiping idols of silver and gold for their comfort.

Where there is sin, there will be punishment because "the wages of sin is death" (Romans 6:23). In the passage above, Isaiah looks beyond the sin of his people to the love and forgiveness of their God. He focuses on repentance and restoration: only turn back to the Lord and He will relent, forgive, and restore. "Though your sins are like scarlet, they shall be as white as snow" (Isaiah 1:18). If Israel persists in its folly, though, then punishment is inevitable. The choice is theirs.

Our time is not much different. We have become, in T. S. Eliot's words, "a decent godless people" or perhaps worse. We, too, have turned to the worship of silver and gold, in the many forms those substances take today. Like Israel of old, we neglect the aged and poor, the marginalized, the broken, and broken hearted. We neglect young women like Kate, who may have had more of a chance in life if someone, anyone, had taken an interest in her. We have justified killing the innocents and profiting from wars and conflicts despite the terrible loss associated with them.

In the last days, though, Isaiah sees better things. All nations will turn to God and He will teach us His ways, not merely so we know what is right, but so we might actually do what is right and pleasing in God's sight. In that day we will *be* His holy people.

But what about Kate and all those like her? Is she simply a lost soul?

At the end of Kate's funeral, a soprano sang "It Is Well with My Soul." I held up the beautiful ceramic urn holding Kate's ashes. The urn had a picture of a butterfly on it, a symbol of transformation. Here is the second verse of the hymn:

"Though Satan should buffet, tho' trials should come,
Let this blessed assurance control,
That Christ has regarded my helpless estate,
And hath shed His own blood for my soul.
It is well, it is well with my soul."

When I heard that, *I knew Kate was safe.* The One whose death and resurrection swallowed up death forever wiped away this young woman's tears, removed her disgrace, and gave her a seat at His banquet.

He is the one for whom we wait. So what do we do now? "Let us walk in the light of the Lord" (Isaiah 2:5).

Prayer
Father of All Mercy, You are Lord of History; all times and people are under Your sovereign sway. You created the human family and have made it beautifully diverse, yet You will that, as diverse as we are, we may be one, even as you are one with the

Son in the unity of the Spirit. You call all people to Your holy mountain where You promise to lavish Your love and abundance upon Your beloved creation when You destroy death forever and wipe the tears from every eye. Bring on the day of your final triumph, and as we wait for the fullness of your promises to be manifest; as we wait for the promise of Jesus' resurrection to be fulfilled, fill us with the Spirit of Jesus so we might wait in joyful hope for his coming as Savior and Lord.

Activity

If there is someone in your family or among your friends who seems lost, reach out to them and let them know you care. But before you do that, pray for them from your heart.

#

Notes

15

Wednesday of the First Week of Advent

Scripture

"In the beginning was the Word, and the Word was with God, and the Word was God. He was with God in the beginning. Through him all things were made; without him, nothing was made that has been made. In him was life, and that life was the light of all mankind. The light shines in the darkness, and the darkness has not overcome it" (John 1:1–5).

Reflection

In the beginning… these words begin the Bible's first book, Genesis, and they begin the gospel of John.

Genesis narrates the story of the first creation, where Adam's disobedience introduced sin, suffering, and death. In stark contrast, the gospel of John presents the new creation, where Jesus' obedience restores life and light to a world that had fallen into darkness. Jesus, the new Adam, redeems God's beloved creation through his perfect obedience.

Jesus, the *Logos*, is not just a human, though he is fully human. He is the divine "Word" who was with God in the beginning and who existed as God with God before the beginning. The Word is the expression of God's creative love, bringing into being everything that will share in His life. Within the inner life of God, the Word is the beloved of the Father, to whom God gives everything He has and is. The Logos, then, *is* God. He perfectly returns the Father's love. Everything the Son has belongs to the Father, and everything the Father has belongs to the Son. In the relationship of Father to Son, we see mutual, perfect self-giving. Thus, Jesus can truthfully say, "Anyone who has seen me, has seen the Father" (John 14:9b). Though distinct, they are perfectly one.

God speaks outside the Godhead through the Logos; through that Word, all things that were made (or ever would be made) come into being, starting with light. Every created thing that is or ever will be exists because of the infinite, loving, and eternal outpouring of divine life spoken at the beginning. We only exist because we have been given a share of the life of the one who reveals Himself as being itself, "I am."

God's first creative word spoken into the formless void of His newly created earth is: "'Let there be light,' and there was light" (Genesis 1:3). That initial light was darkened by sin, tarnished by man's disobedience and selfishness.

In the Word, light returns to the created universe in Jesus, the Word made flesh, born in Bethlehem of the Virgin Mary. Though fully human, he was also fully divine. Jesus restores life because he is the author of life; he is light in the world because he is the light *of* the world, enlightening all humankind. He is the light of life that never dies; His light was not, will not, and cannot be overcome by darkness.

Prayer
Lord, You are the light of the world. Enlighten me today as I seek to do Your will and see Your face. Open my eyes to the beauty of Your created world and the blessings You pour into my life every moment. Give me a grateful heart for Your gifts, great and small. May I always walk as a child of Your light, and may I also reflect Your light in what I say and do, today and every day, You give me the gift of life. I make this prayer in Your Holy Name. Amen.

Activity
In your spiritual journal (if you're not keeping one, this is a good time to start), reflect on Jesus, the Light shining in the darkness of our world. God's promise is that no darkness can ever

overcome the Light of Christ. How do you see that light making inroads into places of darkness? Who are the angels of light who bring the light of the Lord to the world or you? Write about what makes those "angels of light" special or effective. How have they changed the world, or how have they changed you? And how can you bring the light shining within you to others? Resolve to do something today, no matter how small, to bring the light to someone needing it.

#

Notes

Thursday of the First Week of Advent

Scripture
"People of Zion, who live in Jerusalem, you will weep no more. How gracious he will be when you cry for help! As soon as he hears, he will answer you. Although the Lord gives you the bread of adversity and the water of affliction, your teachers will be hidden no more; with your own eyes, you will see them. Whether you turn to the right or the left, your ears will hear a voice behind you, saying, 'This is the way; walk in it'" (Isaiah 30:19–21).

Reflection
My friend, Ed was for a long time, the attorney at the University of Tennessee, Knoxville. Ed had a wonderful sense of humor and a classic Irish wit, but he was also a no-nonsense attorney and a brilliant one at that. Early on in his tenure at UT, he found himself not feeling well on his drive to work. He confided as much to his boss, the university president, who happened to be a physician. The president took one look at him and had Ed rushed to the University of Tennessee Medical Center where he was admitted, subjected to a battery of tests, and told he had to have emergency brain surgery that day to remove a brain tumor.

As Ed waited to be taken to surgery, for the first time in his life he was scared and felt very alone. Then, as he told me the story months later, Ed said he heard a voice, as clear as any voice he had ever heard, as clear as my voice as we talked about this experience months later. The voice said: "Ed, I am with you, I have always been with you, and I will never leave you."

Though we may experience difficult times in our lives, we must never doubt we have been created by a loving God who is always present to us, hears us when we cry out to Him and answers us with love. He speaks to us, not always as clearly as He spoke to Ed, but if we listen, we will hear him calling us to follow Him as His Spirit guides us through life. The Lord doesn't only want us to know he is present, He also wants us to walk in His ways, to bring Good News to those who need it most: to the sick, the suffering, the despised, the lonely, the lost. When we care for the least of our brothers and sisters, we are both hearing His call and walking in His ways.

Prayer

Creator God, You love us beyond all measure. You will that we should live lives rich in the joy of Your presence. When we stray from the path of Your righteousness, You call out to us. You even use the bread of adversity and the water of affliction to bring us back to the path of Your righteousness. Hear our cry for help and forgive our sins so that we might hear Your voice, walk in Your ways, and experience Your gracious love. Amen.

Activity

Make a commitment to help out regularly in a soup kitchen or at a meal offered to people who are in need.

#

Notes

23

Friday of the First Week of Advent

Scripture

"In the sixth month of Elizabeth's pregnancy, God sent the angel Gabriel to Nazareth, a town in Galilee, to a virgin pledged to be married to a man named Joseph, a descendant of David. The virgin's name was Mary. The angel went to her and said, 'Greetings, you who are highly favored! The Lord is with you.' Mary was greatly troubled by his words and wondered what kind of greeting this might be. But the angel said to her, 'Do not be afraid, Mary; you have found favor with God. You will conceive and give birth to a son, and you are to call him Jesus. He will be great and will be called the Son of the Most High. The Lord God will give him the throne of his father David, and he will reign over Jacob's descendants forever; his kingdom will never end.'

'How will this be,' Mary asked the angel, 'since I am a virgin?'

The angel answered, 'The Holy Spirit will come on you, and the power of the Most High will overshadow you. So the holy one to be born will be called the Son of God. Even Elizabeth, your relative is going to have a child in her old age, and she who was said to be unable to conceive is in her sixth month. For no word from God will ever fail.'

'I am the Lord's servant,' Mary answered. 'May your word to me be fulfilled.' Then the angel left her" (Luke 1:26–38).

Reflection

It is hard to imagine how improbable the story of Mary's call would be to the ears of people who had not grown-up calling Mary the Blessed Mother (a title which comes, by the way, from this passage of the gospel of Luke). God's ways are certainly not like our ways.

Mary, as we meet her in this story, is a teenager living in a backwater village in Galilee, which itself was a region of Judea, at the time a despised province of the Roman Empire. If the three most important things about real estate are "location, location, location," the Lord picked a pretty insignificant place to begin the saving work of His Messiah. Yet such are the ways of the Lord.

If the setting is insignificant, so is Mary. She is likely little more than a child of thirteen or fourteen; she is a woman in a patriarchal society and is betrothed to a man named Joseph in a marriage arranged by her parents; probably, she was also illiterate. There is, in short, nothing that distinguishes her or makes her the likely candidate for the future Queen of Heaven, yet that is how God saw her. And for a moment, the future of God's plan for salvation rested on the response Mary would make to the Lord's request.

Mary has found favor with God, the angel tells her. Why might that be so? While she must have been a nice girl, we have no way of knowing why God chose her over all the other nice girls in Judea. But God chooses as He chooses; He is a God of election. While it's pointless to wonder why God chooses as He does, it is wise to note, as Paul would in His letter to the Corinthians, "God chose the weak things of the world to shame the strong" (1 Corinthians 1:27b).

Mary was troubled by all this.

Troubled? She is likely frightened and confused. Gabriel's "don't be afraid," while somewhat reassuring, still left Mary in the dark about what the visit was all about until the angel got to the heart of the matter: You will conceive and bear a son, he will be God's own son as well as yours. You will name him *Jesus* which means "The Lord Saves. He will be the long-awaited Messiah and will sit on David's throne forever.

That's a lot for a teenage girl who can neither read nor write to wrap her head around. She had one question, though: "How can this be since I'm a virgin?"

Gabriel had an answer that required faith: this will all be done by the power of the Holy Spirit. Your son will be known as not only your son but also as God's son. God does amazing things, improbable things, and sometimes impossible things. Your cousin Elizabeth, well beyond childbearing years, is with child. Nothing is impossible for God.

For just one moment even the angels held their breath waiting for Mary's response. She could have said no; the Lord gave her free will after all. She was, however, a little girl with a great heart and great faith. She loved the Lord and wanted to serve him even though she didn't quite understand the mission. "May your word to me be fulfilled." Yes, whatever you want, Lord, I want.

And so, Mary became, for all of us, the prototype of our mission as a church: like her, we have also been called to bring the presence of Jesus, the Lord Who Saves, to the world. We, too, give birth to Him by saying yes to God when he calls to us, and by following the path he lays out for us in every action of our lives.

Prayer
Lord God, we praise You for the faith of Your daughter Mary, the woman who accepted Your invitation to be the mother of Christ, Your Anointed One. May we honor her as the Queen of Heaven, which she is. We are grateful for her obedience and for

the care she had for her son and Yours as He grew in age, wisdom, and grace. Give us obedient hearts so that we might be Your servants and do Your will, even when we don't quite know where You are leading us. Amen

Activity
Read the first chapter of Luke's gospel slowly and prayerfully.

#

Notes

Saturday of the First Week of Advent

Scripture

"Jesus went through all the towns and villages, teaching in their synagogues, proclaiming the good news of the kingdom, and healing every disease and sickness. When He saw the crowds, He had compassion for them because they were harassed and helpless, like sheep without a shepherd. Then He said to his disciples, 'The harvest is plentiful, but the workers are few. Ask the Lord of the harvest, therefore, to send out workers into his harvest field'" (Matthew 9:35–38).

Reflection

Jesus' ministry ushered in the dawn of the Messianic age. He both taught and healed: His teaching about the Kingdom of God which He taught was "in your midst," or "within you." In the incarnation of Jesus, God had indeed drawn near, and with the gift of the Holy Spirit, *we* become God's temple. God's presence is truly within us, the heart of our hearts, nearer to us than we are to ourselves.

This is the unique message of Christianity: Christians have faith that in Jesus we see everything we can possibly know about God in the human form of Christ. Jesus was born a man and shares completely in our human condition: He laughed, cried, loved, wept. Sometimes He was cold, tired, or lonely. He shared our limitations: He needed to learn and grow from childhood to manhood. In all this, He embodied the presence of the divine in human form.

Jesus came to bring the good news that God desired to do for us what we could never do for ourselves: He came to save us. That is the meaning of His name, Jesus (Yeshua), "the Lord Saves."

There is much in a name, at least in that Holy Name. Only Jesus can forgive us and reconcile us to each other and the Father. He does that by obediently taking on our sins and dying for us on the cross: the sinless one in place of the sinner.

Saying the Kingdom is near is one thing, showing it is something else, yet that is exactly what Jesus did: he healed, he restored sight to the blind, he cast out demons. All to show that the Messianic age had dawned. God was breaking into history to redeem and save every last person, especially the harassed and helpless who acted "like sheep without a shepherd." That's a powerful image. Sheep are defenseless animals. They have no way to fight off an attack and need shepherds for protection against predators. Sheep are helpless in other ways too: they need help finding food and water, for example. They are prone to wander and so need to be gathered, sometimes with the aid of a sheepdog.

There was so much work to be done, so many lost souls who needed a compassionate shepherd. Jesus' solution is first, prayer. Ask the Lord of the harvest to send workers into His field. It is, after all, the Lord's harvest, and it's the Lord's lost sheep. We can be of help, like a good sheepdog, but the first and most important action we must take is prayer.

Danielle works for my dog groomer and has always been pleasant and nice, a joy to know. Today I bumped into her at a diner near where she does her grooming. We started talking, and our conversation drifted to a place where I felt I could ask her if she went to any church. She didn't. Danielle grew up Catholic and somewhere along the line she simply dropped out of practicing religion of any kind.

Taking a leap of faith of my own, I invited her to join us in our church on Sunday, but I got a pretty definitive "no thanks, that's not me anymore." Those weren't exactly her words, but you get the gist. After my evangelical failure, I felt pretty low and a little foolish. I shouldn't have, but I did. Then I started writing about the above passage from Matthew's gospel and it was as if the Lord put it on the page just for me. My initial instinct was right; I had compassion for someone whom I sensed needed to know Jesus better. She's part of that great harvest that needs to be brought in; she's a sheep without a shepherd, in great danger from spiritual predators, and in need of the nourishment of faith.

I wasn't the right person to help her but listen to what the Lord tells people like me: pray. Pray to the Lord of the harvest. He loves Danielle, she is His sheep, and what I can do is pray that the Lord will put the right laborer into the field to bring Danielle safely to Him and the Kingdom.

Prayer
Creator God, the harvest is indeed ripe for picking: the harvest of salvation. And your sheep are scattered, hungry, and in danger. Your Son will be returning soon, though we do not know exactly when, but when He does come we, your children, must be ready to go out and greet Him with joy. Lord, send more laborers into your fields to heal the suffering, bind up the wounds of the wounded, comfort the fearful, and bring good news to all. We ask this in the name of the One who died and who now lives as Lord and Christ with You and the Holy Spirit. You are One God forever. Amen.

Activity
Pray today, asking the Lord to send more laborers into his fields to bring in the ripe harvest of salvation.

#

Notes

34

Second Sunday of Advent

Scripture
"Comfort, comfort my people,
says your God.
    Speak tenderly to Jerusalem,
    and proclaim to her
that her hard service has been completed,
that her sin has been paid for,
that she has received from the Lord's hand
double for all her sins.
    A voice of one calling:
'In the wilderness prepare
the way for the Lord;
make straight in the desert
a highway for our God.
    Every valley shall be raised up,
every mountain and hill made low;
the rough ground shall become level,
the rugged places a plain.
    And the glory of the Lord will be revealed,
and all people will see it together.
For the mouth of the Lord has spoken'" (Isaiah 40:1–5).

Reflection
While in Saskatoon to celebrate a wedding some years ago,
I had the pleasure of dining in the home of the groom's elderly
mother. In our conversation, she shared her childhood memories
of the first-ever visit of a reigning monarch to Saskatoon in 1939.
It was an exciting time, one that she would never forget. The
entire province readied itself to welcome King George VI and

Queen Mary. School choirs prepared special songs of welcome, children presented flowers to the King and Queen, the province repaired roads and planted flowers and shrubs along the route of the King's entourage, Saskatoon's downtown was decorated with flags, and the British colors and patients from the Saskatoon sanitarium were wheeled outside to see the royal couple pass by.

We, too, are waiting for the King! We, too, should prepare to welcome Him when He comes.

We await the King of Heaven, of whom Isaiah speaks in the above verse, as Isaiah's prophesy turns from warning to hope.

Yes, God's people had failed over and over again to keep their promises to the Lord. They turned to princes for their safety and forgot the only real safety comes from our God. The prophet foretold the punishment that inevitably flows from unfaithfulness: Israel would suffer. The King of Heaven, however, never forgets His subjects; God never forgets His covenant promises. There will, from time to time, be punishment, but that punishment is never unto death, rather, it is focused on bringing Israel back into the comfort of God's love. Francis Thompson asks of the troubles in his own life: "Is my gloom, after all, / Shade of his hand, outstretched caressingly?"

The King we wait for brings comfort to his people. The Hebrew word for comfort in this passage is *na ham*, and it connotes consoling someone experiencing grief or sadness. The prophet says that God's suffering people will be consoled by nothing less than the coming among them of God Himself. So, the Lord instructs His prophet, "Speak tenderly," that is, speak to the heart, speak to the very core of God's people and each of them, to the place where guilt, fear, doubt, and hopelessness take root. Speak this message into the hearts and minds of God's people: all is forgiven, payment has been made for your transgressions on your behalf. You don't have to come to God; no, God is coming to you, and when He comes, the Glory of the Lord will be revealed to *all* flesh. This is a universal promise of reconciliation and restoration.

So, we must spiritually prepare for the coming of the Lord. How can we make the highway of our hearts ready except by repenting for our sins and failures to welcome God and do His will? We welcome God when we give Him priority in our lives, when we love God with all our being: heart, mind, and strength, and when we love our neighbors as ourselves. We remove the obstacles that may keep us from receiving the great gift God is giving us by forgiving from the heart and by loving even our enemies. We do God's will when we care for His beloved little ones: the sick, the poor, the brokenhearted, and the lonely.

Prayer

Lord, make us ready to receive Your Spirit. You speak tenderly to us, You speak to our hearts, and You tell us how much You love us. Your love for us is greater than our sinfulness, it is greater than our failures, and it is greater than our fears. For this, we should never stop thanking You. Jesus, Your Son, has done for us what we can hardly imagine. He has taken on our human nature, our flesh, and our blood, and He has shown us what it is like to be fully human and to be fully in tune with Your divine will and plan. So, make us ready. Remove the obstacles of our bad habits and selfish ways and make us ready to receive Your Son when He comes in glory to bring healing, to wipe the tears from all faces, and to usher in the new creation. We ask this through Jesus and in the power of the Spirit, with You they are One God forever. Amen.

Activity

Prepare for the Lord's coming by fasting—not from food (unless you'd prefer to do that, and if you do make sure to speak to your physician first), but from other things. Why not fast from TV and Facebook and being glued to your smart devices?

#

Notes

39

Monday of the Second Week of Advent

Scripture

"The desert and the parched land will be glad; the wilderness will rejoice and blossom. Like the crocus, it will burst into bloom; it will rejoice greatly and shout for joy. The glory of Lebanon will be given to it, the splendor of Carmel and Sharon; they will see the glory of the Lord, the splendor of our God. Strengthen the feeble hands, steady the knees that give way; say to those with fearful hearts, 'Be strong, do not fear; your God will come, he will come with vengeance; with divine retribution, he will come to save you'" (Isaiah 35:1–4).

Reflection

A desert can be a desolate and dangerous place. You can lose your way, or even your life, if you don't know how to maneuver the landscape with all its dangers. Water, so essential to life, is in scant supply there; dangerous creatures of every kind stalk, slither and slink through its sands and rock.

Isaiah uses the desert as a metaphor for the barren wasteland that our spiritual world becomes apart from God. There, too, we can lose our way, because without Him there is no compass, there is no path, and there is no rescue. Without Him there is no hope; no way out of the morass of our world when it is separated from its creator.

God keeps His word; when He promises He will come and rescue His people from their sin, He will indeed save. Jesus is the ultimate fulfillment of that promise. The incarnation was the critical part of the Father's plan to rescue not only the Jews but all of His beloved creation. Fully God and fully man, Jesus carried the sins and suffering of the world and did for us what we could never do for ourselves—atone for our sinfulness and reconcile us with the Father. In doing so, He creates in us a holy people, set apart to continue His saving work until He comes again to usher in the final victory of God and goodness over Satan and evil—and take us to be with Him in heaven forever.

God is acting with power in His world—through His Christ and His holy people. It is already bursting into bloom, though we may not see it if we are not looking. Like that crocus bursting into bloom, it comes suddenly and surprises us by heralding the new life of springtime. So it is with God's action among us. If we look, we will see the glory of the Lord giving hope and strength to His people in the direst of circumstances. His glory shines when his people strengthen feeble hands with loving tenderness. It shines when the weak are strengthened by brothers and sisters who care. When people fear the worst, God's glory gives the good news that He will triumph over evil. Sin and death may have their day, but our God has come in our Christ to save us, and He will come again, just as He promised.

Be strong, fear not, your God has come and will come again, He will trample evil, destroy death, and save His beloved people and, indeed, all creation. Then the glory of the Lord will be seen by all peoples.

Prayer
Father, we live in a parched and arid spiritual environment. All around us, people have forgotten your name, abandoned your worship, and ignored your laws. Silver, gold, and power have again taken your place as the objects of devotion. Save us from evil around us and within us. Through Your Spirit, help us strengthen each other with love and share our witness of your power alive in our lives. We ask this in the name of the One who came and is coming. He is lord with You in unity with the Holy Spirit. Amen.

Activity

Reflect on the things that cause you fear or anxiety. Bring those things to the Lord in prayer. Be honest, speak to the Lord as you would speak to your brother, for that is who He is. Ask His help in overcoming your doubts and give Him the burdens you are carrying. This is what He has come to do—to carry our burdens and rescue us from all that threatens us.

#

Notes

Tuesday of the Second Week of Advent

Scripture

"One day Jesus was teaching, and Pharisees and teachers of the law were sitting there. They had come from every village of Galilee, Judea, and Jerusalem. And the power of the Lord was with Jesus to heal the sick. Some men came carrying a paralyzed man on a mat and tried to take him into the house to lay him before Jesus. When they could not find a way to do this because of the crowd, they went up on the roof and lowered him on his mat through the tiles into the middle of the crowd, right in front of Jesus.

"When Jesus saw their faith, he said, 'Friend, your sins are forgiven.'

"The Pharisees and the teachers of the law began thinking to themselves, 'Who is this fellow who speaks blasphemy? Who can forgive sins but God alone?'

"Jesus knew what they were thinking and asked, 'Why are you thinking these things in your hearts? Which is easier: to say, "Your sins are forgiven," or to say, "Get up and walk"? But I want you to know that the Son of Man has authority on earth to forgive sins.' So he said to the paralyzed man, 'I tell you, get up, take your mat, and go home.' Immediately he stood up in front of them, took what he had been lying on, and went home praising God. Everyone was amazed and gave praise to God. They were filled with awe and said, 'We have seen remarkable things today'" (Luke 5:17–26).

Reflection

Jewish tradition considers the parting of the Red Sea to be the greatest of miracles, greater than all the other miracles recounted in the Hebrew Bible. At that time, every one of the Jews rescued by God could look up and see the wonder of the parted waters and rejoice in the power and the love of Yahweh.

In the book *God Was in This Place, & I, I Did Not Know*, author, Lawrence Kushner tells the story of two Jews escaping Egypt and, who completely missed the point, and the beauty of God's action in their lives. As the story goes, once God parted the sea, the seabed was safe to traverse but it wasn't completely dry. These two Jews, Reuven and Shimon, complained about the mud and the slime as they crossed to freedom. They complained continually as they crossed the sea going from slavery to freedom. They never looked up to see the wonder that God was performing. They didn't understand why their fellow Israelites were shouting for joy on the opposite shore.

For Reuven and Shimon, there was no miracle.

Jesus, in the passage above, is surrounded by His critics, lots of them. The Pharisees and Torah scholars had come from far and wide to sit with Jesus, watch Him, and listen to Him with critical ears. But they hadn't come prepared for what they would see: a manifestation of the healing and restoring power of the Spirit of God. They weren't prepared to see a clear sign that the Messianic age had dawned. Even though the power of God was upon Jesus to heal the sick, these critics had not come to be impressed, nor had they come to learn or be healed themselves. They simply watched with jaundiced eyes ready to criticize the young rabbi whose reputation as a healer was spreading rapidly throughout Judea.

Others came, though, who had faith in the Healer from Nazareth, and they were prepared to go to great lengths to bring a paralyzed friend to Jesus' attention. Unable to wade through the crowd of critics, they removed roof tiles and lowered their friend into the room where the Lord was teaching. Then came the miracle of healing: Jesus "saw their faith; he said 'Friend, your sins are forgiven.'"

One would think that the paralytic would have wanted to be cured of his paralysis, but the Lord always heals first what needs healing most. The One who reads the hearts of men knew that forgiveness of this man's sins was his deepest and most important need.

Only God can forgive sin, though, so those fussy lawyers and Pharisees started to grumble in their hearts about the Lord's "blasphemy." How could this young upstart presume to forgive sin? Outrageous, or so it seemed to them.

Knowing His critics' hearts, Jesus addressed their disbelief: is it easier, He said, to forgive sin or to tell a paralyzed man to walk? To demonstrate His power to forgive sin He told the man to get up and walk, and the man did so immediately and went home praising God. Luke tells us "Everyone was amazed and gave praise to God." Everyone!

Everyone who saw this miracle gave praise. Something awesome had happened in their sight. Those who weren't looking for or expecting God's wonders to occur, however, went home grumbling, like Shimon and Reuven traversing the Red Sea. For those grumblers, the lawyers and Pharisees, there was no miracle—to see a miracle requires both faith and insight.

And for us? What does this passage ask of us? It asks us to look for the miracles of faith that occur all around us and be grateful for them. The cry of a newborn child, the kindness of a stranger, the providential meetings that change our lives and our history. All these, and more, cry out for us to give praise and thanks to God.

Activity
Make a list of the miracles of God's love that are in your life today. Tell the Lord in prayer that you are grateful.

#

Notes

49

Wednesday of the Second Week of Advent

Scripture

This is what the Lord says—
your Redeemer, the Holy One of Israel:
"I am the Lord your God,
who teaches you what is best for you,
who directs you in the way you should go.
If only you had paid attention to my commands,
your peace would have been like a river,
your well-being like the waves of the sea.
Your descendants would have been like the sand,
your children like its numberless grains;
their name would never be blotted out
nor destroyed from before me" (Isaiah 48:17–19).

Reflection

Regret is a terrible thing because when we regret something, there has been an irreversible mistake, sometimes small, often huge. If only I had listened to my parents when they told me to study harder or be more careful in choosing my friends. If only I had listened to my doctor telling me to lose weight, eat healthier meals, and exercise. "If only" implies I didn't do what I wish I had done and have suffered the consequences of bad grades, bad friends, or poor health. There is a wistfulness in "if only." We have chosen badly and cannot go back and correct our path. Would that it was different, but it wasn't and now can't be.

Parents are no strangers to the phrase either. They, too, wish their children had made better choices. In Isaiah 48 we see God also wishes His children followed a different path. If only you listened to Me, to My commands, to My Law, to My prophets instead of running amok in the ways of the world. However, God's

51

"if only" is different because He is not only the creator and Father of His people but He is also the Redeemer and Holy One. He is different because He can help us right our wrongs and change our errant ways.

God continues to teach His people through His prophets, His Spirit, and His Word. His teachings are true; they lead to peace within our souls and in the world. Only in His truth can we find joy and life eternal. Every moment of every day, God shows us the path we should take in life. We must discern that path and then choose to travel it.

But we must *listen* to the voice of the Lord, which means taking the time to quiet our spirits and attend to the One who alone can show us the path of life. If we don't hear Him clearly, pray for discernment. Try praying Samuel's prayer in 1 Samuel 3:10, "Speak, for your servant is listening." Or perhaps the prayer we find placed on the lips of Jesus by the author of Hebrews: "Here I am… I have come to do your will, my God" (Hebrews 10:7).

Then wait, watch, and listen with the expectation the Lord will answer that prayer. Somehow, in the silence of your heart or the events of your life, the Lord will speak. If you're unsure of the message, find a spiritually mature fellow Christian, perhaps your pastor or spiritual director, and discuss the matter with him or her.

If you listen for His voice and follow where He is calling you, He will be true to His promises. Your peace will be like a river, your well-being like the waves of the sea. That's a promise.

Prayer
Lord, You speak to us in the silence of our hearts, but we need to slow ourselves down and listen for Your voice, which often seems like a whisper, easily drowned out by the tumult of

our times and the chaos of our lives. Give us ears to hear You and a willingness to do Your will, no matter what You ask of us, regardless of the cost. We ask this in Jesus' name and through the power of the Spirit; with You, they are One God. Amen.

Activity

Set aside some time this evening, sit quietly, slow down your thoughts, and listen for the voice of the Lord to speak to you. As you sit quietly, breathe in and out. With each in-breath, pray, "Here I am, Lord." As you breathe out, pray, "I have come to do Your will." Do this for at least fifteen minutes.

Notes

54

Thursday of the Second Week of Advent

Scripture
"To what can I compare this generation? They are like children sitting in the marketplaces and calling out to others:

    'We played the pipe for you,
and you did not dance;
we sang a dirge,
and you did not mourn.'

For John came neither eating nor drinking, and they say, 'He has a demon.' The Son of Man came eating and drinking, and they say, 'Here is a glutton and a drunkard, a friend of tax collectors and sinners.' But wisdom is proved right by her deeds" (Matthew 11:16–19).

Reflection
You can't please everyone.

Jesus' relationship with his cousin John is complex. They are very different, yet they complement one another. John was an ascetic who ate locusts and wild honey; he sought out the loneliness of the desert to enter into communion with God. John dressed in a manner reminiscent of the prophet Elijah, in camel's hair with a leather belt around his waist. John's enemies, who would later be Jesus' enemies, accused John of being demon-possessed because of his diet and demeanor.

You can't please everyone.

The only One John cared about pleasing was the God who called and sent him to prepare the way for Christ. John was the "voice of one calling: 'In the wilderness prepare the way for the Lord'" (Isaiah 40:3). Malachi prophesied, "See, I will send Elijah to you before the great and terrible day of the Lord comes" (Malachi 4:5). John was the new Elijah, come to prepare the way for the Lord in the wilderness. He dressed and ate as he did all to serve his prophetic calling. He was Elijah who came to prepare for the one who was greater and more powerful than him. The one whose sandal he was unworthy of carrying. Serving God and fulfilling his calling was all that mattered to John. What others thought didn't matter.

John was a prophet in a land that had not heard the voice of prophecy in almost five hundred years. When he appeared on the banks of the Jordan River, he drew great crowds wanting to see this new thing the Lord was doing. His message was simple: "Repent, the kingdom of heaven has come near" (Matthew 3:2).

If John was the advance man and opening act, Jesus was the headliner.

Their messages were identical. Jesus preached: "Repent, for the kingdom of heaven has come near" (Matthew 4:17). There was an urgency in their voices. God was stirring among His people, and great things were already happening. God's reign had begun! So, turn back to him with your heart and soul, with your whole being. Hold nothing back; make nothing more important than turning to the One who came with salvation and love for all people. The One who came with good news!

Jesus' style was different than John's, though. Jesus usually dressed and ate normally but with a difference. In a culture where people only reclined at the table with dear friends, Jesus ate and drank with tax collectors and sinners to such an extent that he was accused of being a "glutton and drunkard" by his enemies.

Like John, Jesus antagonized the self-righteous and religiously smug with his love for outcasts, sinners, the poor and broken, the sick and lost. Jesus and John both preached that God loved those people and longed to have them return to the Father's love. Theirs, too, was the kingdom of heaven.

You can't please everyone.

Jesus knew he didn't have to please everyone. He only had to be obedient to the Father, and that's what He was, "obedient unto death, death on the cross" (Phil. 2:8).

And so, to all His critics and John's as well, Jesus teaches, "Wisdom is proved right by her deeds" (Matt. 11:19). What were Jesus' deeds? Through His ministry, the blind saw, the crippled were healed, the lepers cleansed, and demons expelled. Jesus transformed the lives of those who came to Him for healing and forgiveness. Jesus still heals, transforms, and saves. This is why, more than two thousand years after His resurrection, we can still affirm with the earliest Christians: Jesus saves!

Prayer

Father, the world makes subtle demands on us: to go along with the crowd, to compromise with evil, to remain silent in the face of popular injustice. We are tempted to try to please everyone, everyone but You. Give us wisdom, Father, and let that wisdom guide our choices and our actions. Give us the courage to resist convenient evil in our quest for popularity or acclaim. Give us the courage to follow Your call and to do Your will no matter what others say, and no matter the cost. Let Your wisdom and truth rule our hearts and guide our actions. We ask this in Jesus' name and through the power of the Spirit. Amen.

Activity

Each of us has, if we reflect on it, a story to tell about how the Lord and our relationship with Him has changed us, transformed us, and led us safely through hard times. Take a half hour or so and find a quiet space to reflect on how the Lord has moved in your life. That story, and there will be more than one, is your testimony of faith, your witness to the power and presence of God. That story, if you share it, can bring others to Jesus and open them to His transforming Spirit.

#

Notes

59

Friday of the Second Week of Advent

Scripture

"As they were coming down the mountain, Jesus instructed them, 'Don't tell anyone what you have seen until the Son of Man has been raised from the dead.' The disciples asked him, 'Why then do the teachers of the law say that Elijah must come first?'

Jesus replied, 'To be sure, Elijah comes and will restore all things. But I tell you, Elijah has already come, and they did not recognize him, but have done to him everything they wished. In the same way, the Son of Man is going to suffer at their hands.' Then the disciples understood that he was talking to them about John the Baptist" (Matthew 17:9–13).

Reflection
What about Elijah? When will he come?

My sister Barbara loved life, and she wanted to live a long, happy one. When she was only fifty-four, though, she was diagnosed with ovarian cancer. Ovarian cancer is deadly in large part because it is difficult to diagnose early. When this stealthy killer shows symptoms, it is often too late to treat it effectively. Barbara only went to the doctor when she lost weight unexpectedly and couldn't fit into her clothes because her abdomen became distended, a classic sign of ovarian cancer. Her cancer, by this time, had already reached stage four.

Chemotherapy soon became ineffective. Barbara stormed heaven, asking the Lord to heal her. She drove from her home in New Jersey to Worcester, Massachusetts, to attend a healing service conducted by Fr. Ralph DiOrio, who was noted for his gift of healing. We prayed with him for Barbara, but seemingly to no avail, the cancer continued to grow.

While Barb's body weakened, her spirit began to soar. She was able to let go of long-held grudges and animosity. She found forgiveness in her heart. She became calmer and more accepting of others. When her daughter Donna flew into New York from Chicago to be with her mom, Donna's boyfriend, Colin, picked her up at the airport and drove her directly to New York University Hospital. While Donna visited, Colin lingered in the waiting room, fearing a visit with my sister, who had made no secret that she disapproved of him.

Knowing Colin was there, Barbara, voice weakened by cancer, asked to see him. He explained he didn't think Barb would want to see him. "Oh no," she explained, "none of that matters anymore," and they embraced. Barbara had indeed been healed, but not in the way she had prayed; God heals us the way we need to be healed, not how we want to be healed.

Jesus' discussion with his disciples about the Messianic role of Elijah reminds us that God does what God does the way God does it, and while it may not always look like His power is in play, make no mistake about it, it is.

Peter had just professed he believed Jesus to be the promised Messiah. That confession of faith did not come without baggage. The disciples thought Jesus would be the Messiah they expected, the one who would defeat the Romans, re-establish David's kingdom, and sit on its throne. They would be disappointed; the Father had a different, better plan.

Jesus affirmed the expectation that Elijah would come and restore all things to prepare for the Messiah. Malachi foresaw the mission of Elijah as one of reconciliation: "He will turn the hearts of the parents to their children and the hearts of the children to their parents, or else I will come and strike the land with total destruction" (Malachi 4:6). In John the Baptist, Elijah comes and has come. He will restore all things, but not as His disciples imagined. Initially, Jesus' disciples would be disappointed, but God had a different, better plan.

John precedes the crucified Messiah in martyrdom. John's ministry is a precursor of Jesus'. Both proclaimed the good news of God's love for all, no exceptions; both antagonized the powers of the privileged elites; the world rejected both, and both were put to death by their enemies. John, indeed, prepared the way for the Lord.

What the world sees as defeat, God sees as victory, the victory of obedience and faith in a plan greater than anything the world has to offer. The world could not defeat God's plan: not in the case of the Baptist, not in the case of the Messiah. Nor can the world defeat God's plan for us. My sister's prayers were heard in ways better than we could imagine. His ways are not ours, nor is His wisdom our wisdom, but in Jesus crucified and risen, we see the power of God and wisdom of God which cannot be overcome, resisted, or thwarted by the powers of this world, not by cancer, not by evil, not by corruption. God wins—no matter how it might look.

Elijah has come, Christ Jesus has come, the victory is won, and in Jesus' cross and resurrection, life triumphs over death forever.

Prayer

Saving Lord, in John the Baptist, Elijah has come to prepare the way for You and Your cross. While the powers of this world seemed to have their way with Him, he succeeded in doing the

Father's will. He lived a life of faithfulness and self-gift that prepared the world for Your sacrificial death on the cross. Help us to see the providential hand of Your Father in all of our struggles and give us faith in your promise that those who live believing in You will never die. We ask this in Your holy name and through the Spirit, with the Father, You are One God. Amen.

Activity

Visit someone you know who is sick or suffering and offer to pray with them. If they are unwilling to pray, pray for them.

Take some quiet time to remember and meditate on a time when you felt God disappointed you. Was there a deeper blessing you might not have been aware of? If you can, be grateful for something you find in your reflection on that disappointment.

#

Notes

65

Saturday of the Second Week of Advent

Scripture
  "The Spirit of the Sovereign Lord is on me
because the Lord has anointed me
to proclaim good news to the poor.
He has sent me to bind up the brokenhearted,
to proclaim freedom for the captives
and release from darkness for the prisoners,
  to proclaim the year of the Lord's favor
and the day of vengeance of our God,
to comfort all who mourn,
  and provide for those who grieve in Zion—
to bestow on them a crown of beauty
instead of ashes,
the oil of joy
instead of mourning,
and a garment of praise
instead of a spirit of despair (Isaiah 61:1–3a).

Reflection
The Messiah is coming with power and salvation. While God's beloved may struggle for a season, they should never struggle without hope, without the assurance that the Anointed One is sent with good news for God's chosen ones.

Isaiah speaks this prophecy to a people newly returned from seventy years of exile in Babylon. In those years, the Jews had seen Jerusalem destroyed and its temple demolished. The monarchy was abolished, and no one would ever again sit on David's throne.

In the time leading up to their exile, many Jews were killed, and in defeat, the best and brightest of Jewish society were taken by force to Babylon. Only the poorest among the people were left to tend to the land.

Now, generations later, Cyrus the Persian, who had conquered Babylon, allowed the Jews to return to their land where they could rebuild their city and God's temple. God had relented in His punishment of a faithless nation, but all did not go smoothly. Only a remnant of the exiles chose to return; the others had assimilated into Babylonian culture. When the remnant returned to Jerusalem, they were overwhelmed by the devastation they found. They were home, but restoring their nation would be very difficult.

To these discouraged people, and to the discouraged of all times in all places, God speaks through the prophet Isaiah, saying help is on the way. The Spirit of the Living God is moving, as he did over the waters at the dawn of creation, and when the Spirit moves, there is always new life. The Spirit has anointed One to come in God's name, to baptize with that same Spirit, and to bring good news to those most in need, to the poor.

Here is what that good news looks like: He will bind up the wounds of the brokenhearted. This is more than bringing consolation; it is healing and repairing the suffering and hurt of those who have been crushed by suffering and sadness. The Anointed of the Lord, the Christ, will not fix, He will utterly transform. Those held captive by their circumstances, or their sins will be free, totally and gloriously free. It will be like going from total darkness to glorious light. For those who mourn, He will bring the news that death itself is defeated, so even when grieving, we can have the joy of knowing that life always triumphs over death. Christ is coming to bring the good news that, by God's grace, we can be totally and utterly transformed and made utterly new.

The prophecy of Isaiah is a prophecy for us too. We are tempted to see our lives with worldly eyes. There are, for us, too, difficulties we must endure and difficult work we must do to restore our own lives, our nation, and our world. It is easy to be discouraged and even overwhelmed. But take courage, and fear not. Help is on the way. The Promised One will come, even as He came. And to the poor (and aren't we all beggars as we stand before God?), He brings the good news of His transforming love. And, until He comes in glory, He commissions us to bring the good news, in His name, to our families, our communities, and even to the ends of the earth.

Prayer
Jesus our Brother, you have been anointed Lord and Christ by your Father in the Spirit. Even now, You are renewing all things by the power of Your love. Renew my heart and make it beat in rhythm with your own sacred heart. Fill us with love for the poor, and who is poorer than the soul who does not know You? Give us the love and the courage to live as your brothers and sisters, filled with joy and peace, so that the world that does not know You yet might see You in us. Through our witness and our lives help the world to know the promised Messiah has come in you and will come again to make all things new.

Activity
Today, find a way to bring good news to the poor. Do you have an elderly relative who may be lonely? Call or (better yet) visit them. Don't forget to bring cookies! Is there someone who

needs to know you love them? Maybe an estranged family member or sibling? Reach out to them with a call or a card. Take the first step. Finally, tell someone whom you love deeply that you love them—and make some gesture of love because people in love make signs of love. Flowers? An evening out? Have fun with this.

#

Notes

Third Sunday of Advent

Scripture

"There was a man sent from God whose name was John. He came as a witness to testify concerning that light so that through him all might believe. He, himself, was not the light; he came only as a witness to the light.

Now this was John's testimony when the Jewish leaders in Jerusalem sent priests and Levites to ask him who he was. He did not fail to confess, but confessed freely, "I am not the Messiah."

They asked him, "Then who are you? Are you Elijah?" He said, "I am not." "Are you the Prophet?" He answered, "No."

Finally, they said, "Who are you? Give us an answer to take back to those who sent us. What do you say about yourself?" John replied in the words of Isaiah the prophet, "I am the voice of one calling in the wilderness, 'Make straight the way for the Lord'" (John 1:6-8,19-23).

Reflection

It is important to know who you are and who you are not.

In the movie *Moonstruck*, we meet Rose, an older woman in an unhappy marriage who is often alone while her faithless husband is off gallivanting. One evening, dining by herself in a restaurant, Rose observes Perry as he is embarrassingly dumped by his date. Rose invites Perry to share a meal with her, which he does. They have a lovely conversation, and after their meal, Perry walks her home. At her home, they hesitate for an awkward moment; Perry expected an invitation to come into her home, but that invitation was not forthcoming. She is a married woman and will be faithful to her husband despite his flaws. Confused, he asked why, and she explained, "Because I know who I am."

John the Baptist had a critical role to play in salvation history: he was sent to be Elijah to prepare the way for God's own Anointed. It was a delicate assignment; his call was not to point to himself but to another. His message of repentance leading to forgiveness of sin was to prepare for the ministry of Jesus. Of his cousin, he would say: "He must become greater; I must become less" (John 3:30). John was a great man, and part of his greatness was his humility before the Lord. John knew who he was!

It must have been tempting for John to believe all his good press! People from Jerusalem and Judea flocked to him in the desert to hear his call to repentance, to confess their sins, and to wash themselves with John's baptism. John gave hope to even the most hopeless Israelite. He was acclaimed as a prophet, the first one heard in the land in almost 500 years. People thought he was the promised messiah, but he ended that talk definitively. He knew who he was.

John wasn't the light that was coming into the world, but he was the Lord's advance man, preparing the crowds to welcome the light when it appeared. John was not the sun, radiating light, but he was the moon, reflecting it! John was the great first witness to Jesus, the light of the world.

Witnesses present evidence through their testimony and otherwise; they speak the truth and point to the truth so that others may know the truth and be set free by that knowledge. And what was the truth the Baptist testified to? It was that in the One who was to come after him light and life would dawn in a land long in darkness. That light would appear in the wilderness, of all places: dangerous, barren, and forbidding. Yet the Lord's path was to be right through the wilderness of sin, of evil, of hatred and oppression. Make straight his path in the wilderness where on the cross Christ would defeat death forever.

John knew who he was—and we must also know who we are!

In the wilderness of our lives, in the disappointments, in the tragedies, in the brokenness, and even in the sin, we must make a straight path for the Lord, who will transform our wilderness and heal our arid spirits. Yet we must know our sins and weaknesses; we must know where all the broken pieces of our lives are hiding before we can make that straight way for the Lord. Only He can restore us, but only we can let Him in.

Know who you are—and make a highway in the wilderness for the Lord who comes.

Prayer
Creating and redeeming Lord, You long to enter the wilderness of our lives to bring us healing, hope, and love. Only You can restore us. We have made a mess of our lives; our sins have tarnished the One in whose Image we were made; our faithlessness has destroyed the joy You long for us to know. Our weaknesses and worldliness pull us away from the happiness we seek in all the wrong places. Today, we turn again to You and, in doing so, reject the glamor and deceit of evil and the Evil One. Let that desire to turn back to You create a highway so Your Holy Spirit might renew and transform us into the people You have made us to be. We make this prayer to You and the Father in and through the Spirit. You are One God forever and ever. Amen.

Activity
In the evening, before bedtime, find a quiet place and do a fierce and fearless examination of your conscience. Where are the

places in your life most in need of the Lord's help and healing? Is there any action the Lord asks you to take to "set things right?" Are there people you need to make amends to? Are there wrongs you can at least partially right? Is there love in your heart you need to express and share? If you answered any of these questions in the affirmative, do what the Lord asks of you, but don't think you're doing it alone. He is with you, He loves you, and He will transform your wilderness with streams of living water.

#

Notes

Monday of the Third Week of Advent

Scripture
"For I, the Lord, love justice,
I hate robbery and wrongdoing.
In my faithfulness, I will reward my people
And make an everlasting covenant with them.
Their descendants will be known among the nations,
and their offspring among the peoples.
All who see them will acknowledge
That they are a people the Lord has blessed.

   I delight greatly in the Lord;
my soul rejoices in my God.
For he has clothed me with garments of salvation
and arrayed me in a robe of his righteousness,
as a bridegroom adorns his head like a priest,
and as a bride adorns herself with her jewels.
   For as the soil makes the sprout come up
and a garden causes sccds to grow,
so the Sovereign Lord will make righteousness
and praise spring up before all nations (Isaiah 61:8–11).

Reflection
Our God is the Lord of history. He is neither remote nor disinterested. Rather, He cares about His people and shows His love in the twists and turns of our lives and stories, both as individuals and as nations. Our choices matter to the Lord; our sin is an abomination in His eyes, and His passion is for our repentance and return to Him. Throughout Scripture, we hear the voice of YHWH inviting His people to repent and return to Him "Even now," declares the Lord, "return to me with all your heart" (Joel 2:12).

The Lord punished Israel's faithlessness with seventy years of exile in Babylon, but that punishment was not for punishment's sake; it was meant to elicit repentance and new life. In Isaiah 61, we hear the Lord speaking to the faithful remnant of His chastened people, newly returned from exile to their land. To them, the Lord speaks words of comfort and hope: "I will reward my people and make an everlasting covenant with them" through the ministry of the coming Anointed One. In His Anointed One, the Messiah, the Lord promises His people will be blessed and that blessedness will testify to *all* people of God's faithfulness and His power to transform even the most defeated and despised of people into a nation radiating new life.

This promise is fulfilled in Jesus, and God's transforming love has embraced the world and everyone in it through Him. We could never save ourselves; we have no righteousness but His! In Him, we have the gift of the Spirit, and that Spirit makes life eternal, emerge from the depths of our being, the life that only God can give. And so we are radically transformed; in Paul's words, we become a "new creation" (2 Corinthians 5:17).

What began in Jesus' life, death, and resurrection will be completed when the Lord comes again, when He will usher in the new creation in its fullness and wipe the tears from every eye. The God who has made these wonderful promises will bring all this to pass, "the one who calls you is faithful!" (1 Thessalonians 5:24).

Prayer

Father, you are Lord of history, and we know that even now, in the darkness of our times, when nations rise against nations and when there are wars and rumors of war around the globe, you are still working all things for the good of your beloved people, whom you have called according to your purposes (Romans 8:28). In our personal lives, when we walk the dark valleys, you walk with us, guiding us like a shepherd and loving us like our dear friend. As we wait for the fullness of Your victory at the end of the ages, give us the confidence to know that in You the victory of Goodness is assured, and we have nothing to fear. Keep us faithful as we wait. We ask this in Jesus' name and through the power of the Spirit, with You they reign over history until the end of the ages. Amen

Activity

Reflect on the world today and on your own story: how do you see the hand of God present in what is going on in the world today? Where has God been active in guiding your life? Have there been times when you felt blessed by God's loving care or chastised for your sin? Where do current events seem to be leading the world? Do you see God's grace and love somehow shining in the darkness? If you keep a journal, and I hope you do, write about these questions and see where your writing leads you.

#

Notes

82

Tuesday of the Third Week of Advent

Scripture

   "The days are coming," declares the Lord,
"when I will raise up for David a righteous branch,
a king who will reign wisely
and do what is just and right in the land.
   In his days Judah will be saved
and Israel will live in safety.
This is the name by which he will be called:
The Lord Our Righteous Savior" (Jeremiah 23:5–6).

Reflection

A cynic once said that the difference between a pessimist and an optimist is that the pessimist says: "Things couldn't get worse," and the optimist replies: "O yes, they can!"

Jeremiah is sometimes called the Weeping Prophet because of his seemingly constant laments. Jeremiah's nation was falling apart, its leaders were corrupt, and its people would soon be scattered into exile due to the Lord's righteous judgment. Yet, according to the above statement, he was an optimist. When it seemed things couldn't get worse, Jeremiah announced YHWH's promise of salvation. Good things were on the way, and the Lord would send His beleaguered people a wise king who would rule with justice and mercy. He would be called Righteous Savior.

God fulfills his promises. He promised David that "I will raise up your offspring to succeed you, your own flesh and blood, and I will establish his kingdom. He is the one who will build a house for my Name, and I will establish the throne of his kingdom forever. I will be his father, and he will be my son" (2 Samuel 7:12b–14a). In Jeremiah, the Lord reiterates his promise to raise up a king from

David's line who would rule wisely, do justice, and rescue God's people. That is the king worth serving.

What David was promised, what Israel hoped for, and what Jeremiah prophesied is fulfilled in the birth of the Lord our righteous Savior, Jesus of Nazareth. He is the One who, through his perfect obedience to the Father, restored not only Israel but all creation. All people have the promise of a new life in Him. He proclaimed not merely the Kingdom of Judah or Israel but that the Kingdom of God is in our midst *now*. It is within you, available to anyone who accepts Jesus as Lord and Savior and lives in obedience to Him and His law of Love.

Prayer
Lord, our Righteous Savior, you invite us to be citizens of the Kingdom of Your Father and to live in that Kingdom now. We commit ourselves to you, our King, Lord, and Savior. Keep us faithful to your will and give us the courage to serve You regardless of the consequences. We ask this of the Father through the Spirit. Amen.

Activity
Jeremiah tells us the Great King will be wise and do what is right and just. As His subjects, we, too, must strive to be wise and to treat others justly and with love. So, today, pray for wisdom and trust that the Lord will give you the wisdom you seek. James writes: "If any of you lacks wisdom, you should ask God, who gives generously to all without finding fault, and it will be given to you. But when you ask, you must believe and not doubt" (James 1:5–6a). Having prayed for wisdom, ask the Lord if there is anything you can do to make the world a more just or loving place. Maybe someone needs to hear words of forgiveness or love from you; be sure to speak them no matter how hard it might be. In all this, give thanks to the Lord.

#

Notes

85

Wednesday of the Third Week of Advent

Scripture

"For God so loved the world that he gave his one and only Son, that whoever believes in him shall not perish but have eternal life. For God did not send his Son into the world to condemn the world, but to save the world through him. Whoever believes in him is not condemned, but whoever does not believe stands condemned already because they have not believed in the name of God's one and only Son. This is the verdict: Light has come into the world, but people loved darkness instead of light because their deeds were evil. Everyone who does evil hates the light and will not come into the light for fear that their deeds will be exposed. But whoever lives by the truth comes into the light so that it may be seen plainly that what they have done has been done in the sight of God" (John 3:16–31).

Reflection

The verdict is in. In John 3, the evangelist uses the language of a courtroom. The trial is over, the judge has deliberated on the guilt or innocence of the accused, and when the verdict is handed down, the accused will be either convicted or exonerated.

The rendering of a verdict is the moment of truth. The truth we find in the third chapter of John is that we are guilty!

We are guilty of loving darkness rather than light, of being addicted to our evil deeds, and of being unwilling to change those habits because they possess us. Sinful, broken humanity and our sinful, broken world are condemned. The sentence is death!

But wait, there's more to the story than the just sentence of God on the world that rejects and betrays Him. He loves this world, in all its sinfulness and evil, sitting, as it is, in darkness and careening toward destruction. God's love for us is unwavering, for He made us, and He made us good. He loves us because we are the creative outpouring of His eternal, infinite love.

The God, who is love, loves the work of his hand, loves it so much that He gave it the ultimate outpouring and expression of His love: Jesus who enfleshes perfectly, infinitely, eternally, the loving self-gift of God. The Father is perfect love, and the Son perfectly reflects and returns that love. In the Son's obedience to the Father, the Son comes before God as the advocate for all humanity; He pleads on our behalf and wins an acquittal by His blood shed for us as an atoning sacrifice on Calvary. This is the depth of God's love for us, a love that can comfort and reassure us in our darkest moments.

We no longer have to live in darkness and evil. The light has come into the world; all we have to do is believe in the One who is the Light of the World, and we will have eternal life. This is not just a promise but an opportunity for salvation that can fill us with hope and inspire us to change our ways.

Prayer
Loving God, You are the source and goal of all life. All life comes from You and returns to You. You made us in Your image—in the image of infinite, eternal, selfless self-gift. Jesus, Your Messiah, shows us the way back to You. In Him we see You, and we know You. He has revealed everything we can know of You, and he lights the way back to You. Fill us with a vibrant belief in Him and His love, as well as Your love. We stand guilty before You, but through faith in Your Son, You commute our death sentence and give us the gift of eternal life. Give us grateful hearts that reflect

Your infinite generosity as images of Your love show us ways to love ourselves every day of our lives. We ask this in Jesus' name and through the power of the Spirit. Together, You are One God forever and ever. Amen.

Activity

In our passage today, we hear that God loves and forgives sinners (us). He does this without any expectation that we have remorse for our sins. In fact, He knows unless He saves us from ourselves, we will be lost. So today, find some way to be gratuitously generous and kind to someone with no other claim on Your generosity than being a person in need. Make it a direct gift, not a donation to an organization. Let this act of love and kindness be "hands-on."

#

Notes

90

Thursday of the Third Week of Advent

"'Though the mountains be shaken
and the hills be removed,
yet my unfailing love for you will not be shaken,
nor my covenant of peace be removed,'
says the Lord, who has compassion on you" (Isaiah 54:10).

Reflection
The world is a mess.

As I write, a deadly war between Ukraine and Russia continues to kill hundreds of thousands of men and women, many innocent victims cavalierly called "collateral damage" in press reports. The Middle East is exploding as Israel struggles to defend itself from the terrorist nations that surround it. Communist China threatens to invade Taiwan. Any one of these international hotspots could ignite a third world war.

Americans themselves have never been more divided. Hatred is used as a political tool as the left uses vilification and character assassination to advance its agenda of total government control of the lives and fortunes of the people the government is meant to serve. More than at any other time in U.S. history, the government of the people, by the people, and for the people, established by our Constitution, may well perish from the earth.

Due to mass illegal immigration over porous borders, whole sections of American cities have been overrun with foreign gangs that terrorize and destroy the nation they have invaded. Rampant inflation steals money from hard-working Americans, and high taxes take even more from the productive classes.

Is it any wonder that people around the world fear for their future?

Isaiah's words of comfort to Israel at a time of similar destruction and uncertainty are a comfort to all of us who worry about what will happen to our world, our nation, our freedom, and our lives. Whatever happens around us, the Lord's love for His people will never be withdrawn; His compassion abides with us. He has made a covenant of love that will never be abolished. Our God keeps the promises He makes and promises us His love and peace forever.

There are no strings attached to the Lord's promise of faithfulness. No matter what is falling apart around us, He is with us. The Good Shepherd does not leave His flock when trouble looms. He walks with us through the darkest and most frightening places, comforting and protecting us.

Our world may be falling apart, and we may see no place to run, no human rescuer. The problems confronting our world and ourselves may seem hopeless. Even though aspects of our world that appear unshakable as the mountains are destroyed before our eyes, the Lord says, "Fear not, for I am with you." Your help does not come from some government, a charismatic leader, or the force of arms. Your help comes from the Lord your God, who loves you and whose compassion never fails.

The Lord promises us his unfailing love and compassion through the darkest moments of our lives or history. He promises that, in the end, life, love, and peace will prevail. The angels' proclamation to the shepherds at Jesus' birth was also the pledge of final victory: there will be peace on earth, and it will come through the Savior, born of Mary in a stable, who would die on a cross and be raised on the third day by the glory of the Father.

He sent us the Spirit to abide with us, and that Spirit will guide us through the most challenging times into the glory and joy of God's Kingdom.

Put your faith in the Lord and His promises, follow where the Spirit leads you, and trust the promise of life made to all who remain faithful through the trials and tribulations of this world.

Prayer
Creating and Redeeming God, Your love for us knows no limits. You promise to be faithful to Your covenant and Your covenant people. Give us faith in that promise. Our world is troubled in many places; we lift it to You and ask You to heal it and us. Heal our world, our nation, our people. Only You know Your plans for us, but we trust they are compassionate and loving. Give us a heart that responds to You with trust and gratitude. Show us the path You want us to walk and give us the courage to walk it knowing that You walk with us. In a troubled world full of wars and rumors of war, make us instruments of Your peace, which surpasses our understanding, Your shalom. We pray this in the Holy Name of Jesus, and through the power of the Spirit, we know that with You, they are One God forever. Amen.

Activity
We shouldn't worry about those things in life over which we have no control. We can pray for those things, though, because all of history is under the sovereignty of God, and God hears the prayers of His beloved children (us). So today, and every day hereafter, pray for the world, for people caught up in the terror of war and hatred, and for the hateful people themselves and their conversion. If you are well enough, fast along with your prayer (but consult your physician before embarking on any fasting program). I have been doing intermittent fasting, which requires you to eat meals within eight hours. For example, I have a modest

breakfast at eight in the morning, then I have a second meal around two thirty in the afternoon, ensuring I finish no later than four o'clock. This regimen allows me to eat healthy meals, but I also deny myself when I get hungry around dinner time.

#

Notes

95

Friday of the Third Week of Advent

Scripture

"And Mary said:
'My soul glorifies the Lord
and my spirit rejoices in God my Savior,
for he has been mindful
of the humble state of his servant.
From now on all generations will call me blessed,
for the Mighty One has done great things for me—
Holy is his name.
His mercy extends to those who fear him,
from generation to generation.
He has performed mighty deeds with his arm;
He has scattered those who are proud in their inmost thoughts.
He has brought down rulers from their thrones
but has lifted up the humble.
He has filled the hungry with good things
but has sent the rich away empty.
He has helped his servant Israel,
remembering to be merciful
to Abraham and his descendants forever,
just as he promised our ancestors'" (Luke 1:46–55).

Reflection

Mary's Canticle, often called the Magnificat, is perhaps the first Christmas carol. It is a song of pure joy in the magnificence of God and His ways among us.

Even as a teenager, the time in life when most of us become self-centered and self-focused, Mary was kind and thoughtful toward others. We can see Mary's compassion while visiting her elderly relative, Elizabeth. The angel had told Mary that Elizabeth, in her old age, was also expecting a child. Nothing, Gabriel reminded Mary, is impossible for God. So, while pregnant, Mary took an arduous journey to visit and care for her cousin Elizabeth.

There is a generational difference in the ages of these two women. Mary has just come of childbearing age, and Elizabeth has experienced menopause. She is probably in her fifties. While they are traditionally considered cousins, Elizabeth is likely Mary's first cousin once removed. Their ages differ by forty or more years. Still, though newly pregnant herself, Mary travels to help Elizabeth as her time to give birth to the one who will grow up to be John the Baptist, draws near.

When Mary arrived at Elizabeth's home, the baby in Elizabeth's womb leaped for joy. The Holy Spirit, the Spirit of Prophesy, came over the older woman who spoke these words: "Blessed are you among women, and blessed is the child you will bear! But why am I so favored, that the mother of my Lord should come to me? As soon as the sound of your greeting reached my ears, the baby in my womb leaped for joy. Blessed is she who has believed that the Lord would fulfill his promises to her!" (Luke 1:42b–45).

These were reassuring words for a girl who was beginning an extraordinary and difficult journey.

Mary broke out in a song of praise to God, a prayer that has been prayed for more than two thousand years by Christians in all parts of the globe.

"My soul glorifies the Lord," she sang, "and my spirit rejoices in God my savior." Why? Not because she was great in the eyes of the world; no, God regarded her in her lowly state because she was a humble, insignificant, but faith-filled young woman. God deserves the honor and praise: the Almighty alone does great things because He and only He is holy. Her God is merciful and mighty, and His ways are not ours. God scatters the proud and deposes kings, but He lifts up and exalts the humble. God feeds the poor and helps them, and aren't we all poor as we stand before Him? The rich are those who think they don't need God because they can rely on themselves; they are the ones who are truly poor, empty, and alone.

God is a lover and promise keeper: He keeps the promises he made to Abraham, He kept the promises He made to Mary, and He will keep the promises He made to us. To Martha, grieving at her brother's tomb, Jesus said: "I am the resurrection and the life. The one who believes in me will live, even though they die; and whoever lives by believing in me will never die" (John 11:25b–26a). This is the promise Mary's Son came to make; he went on to ask Martha, and through her, us: "Do you believe this?"

Now, that is a promise to sing about! May all our souls magnify this saving and life-giving Lord! May our spirits rejoice in Jesus, our Lord and Savior. God *is* with us.

Prayer
Saving Lord, let us magnify Your glory and love every moment of our lives, and may we rejoice in Your saving love, never ceasing to thank and praise You for Your gift of saving love. You called Mary to be Your mother, she is the one who intimately taught You, the Logos, how to speak. Her humility is an image of your own willingness to take on our human flesh, assuming the likeness of a slave. Help us to be Your humble servants, and let our lives

give witness to Your good news. We ask this in your name and through the Spirit, with the Father, you are One God. Amen.

Activity
Read, slowly and prayerfully, Mary's Song. Pray it with her.

\#

Notes

Saturday of the Third Week of Advent

Scripture

"I will send my messenger, who will prepare the way before me. Then suddenly the Lord you are seeking will come to his temple; the messenger of the covenant, whom you desire, will come," says the Lord Almighty.

But who can endure the day of his coming? Who can stand when he appears? For he will be like a refiner's fire or a launderer's soap. He will sit as a refiner and purifier of silver; he will purify the Levites and refine them like gold and silver. Then the Lord will have men who will bring offerings in righteousness, and the offerings of Judah and Jerusalem will be acceptable to the Lord, as in days gone by, as in former years" (Malachi 3:1–4).

Reflection

"Be careful what you wish for." Sage advice! When we wish for success in our chosen career, we may achieve it at an unforeseen cost. Our wished-for success may come with greater responsibilities that will take us away from time with our family. The result is less happiness than we might have otherwise had. My stepson Patrick was wise at a young age. As a teenager, he wished for a comfortable life, but he didn't want great wealth. "Wealthy people have more problems," he observed. "I want normal problems." Now in his forties, Patrick is living a comfortable life with normal problems, and he is as happy as one can expect to be on this side of eternity.

In the passage above, Malachi writes to the Jews who returned from exile in Babylon. It has now been several decades since their return, and they are not happy about the conditions in their homeland. They rebuilt the Lord's temple with tremendous effort and expected their God to return and make His home among men there again, but they saw no evidence of His return home.

They also have some traditional complaints: the good suffer, the wicked prosper. What's that all about? Where, they ask, is the God of justice? They wish that God would return bringing justice to the land.

Be careful what you wish for.

And so, the Lord speaks: I am coming, make no mistake about it. And I send my messenger ahead of me to prepare the way. The preparation for the arrival of the King would require fixing the roads over which he would travel, but the prophet suggests a different kind of repair: the repair of the soul! We must repent to prepare for the coming of the righteous One before whom all sins, even those we consider minor, are an abomination.

Our preparation will require a fierce and honest personal and communal examination of conscience. As individuals and as a nation, how have we comported our thoughts, actions, and decisions to the righteousness of God? Have we put God's ways ahead of our own? Have we chosen our plan for life considering God's plan, or have we selfishly wished to achieve our own desires?

Be careful what you wish for.

YHWH, whose coming His people wished for, comes suddenly, unexpectedly. But who can endure it? The day of the Lord will not be cheap grace. The Lord comes to refine and purify His people. The refining process for metal is hot and dangerous. Metal is heated in the refiner's fire and the pure alloy sinks to the bottom of the cauldron while impurities surface to the top to be removed and thrown away. So the Lord, when He comes, will separate the pure from the impure. The purified ones will again live in the light of the Lord, but the impure will face God's justice and judgment.

The purpose of the Lord's coming is to purify and restore, not to punish. The time of His coming will be difficult, but for those who seek refuge in Him, it will be a great day of restoration and return.

Come, Lord Jesus!

Prayer
Lord Jesus Christ, as You once came to us as Mary's child in Bethlehem, we await Your return in power to again dwell among us. We know that Your day of return will be a time of justice and reckoning, but we also know that You love us, and You will come, as You once came, with love and salvation for Your people. Keep us faithful as we wait for that day, and when You come, may You find us with our lamps lit and ready to welcome You home. May Your Kingdom come. Amen.

Activity
With pen in hand, conduct a fierce and honest personal and communal examination of conscience. As individuals and as a nation, how have we comported our thoughts, actions, and decisions to the righteousness of God? How might we do better, and what must we repent? Write all this down as a reminder and periodically return to it to assess your spiritual progress.

#

Notes

Fourth Sunday of Advent

Scripture
"A shoot will come up from the stump of Jesse;
from his roots a Branch will bear fruit.
   The Spirit of the Lord will rest on him—
the Spirit of wisdom and of understanding,
the Spirit of counsel and of might,
the Spirit of the knowledge and fear of the Lord—
   and he will delight in the fear of the Lord.
   He will not judge by what he sees with his eyes,
or decide by what he hears with his ears;
   but with righteousness he will judge the needy,
with justice he will give decisions for the poor of the earth.
He will strike the earth with the rod of his mouth;
with the breath of his lips he will slay the wicked.
   Righteousness will be his belt
and faithfulness the sash around his waist.
   The wolf will live with the lamb,
the leopard will lie down with the goat,
the calf and the lion and the yearling together;
and a little child will lead them.
   The cow will feed with the bear,
their young will lie down together,
and the lion will eat straw like the ox.
   The infant will play near the cobra's den,
and the young child will put its hand into the viper's nest.
   They will neither harm nor destroy
on all my holy mountain,
for the earth will be filled with the knowledge of the Lord
as the waters cover the sea" (Isaiah 11:1–9).

Reflection

How different that is from what we experience today. A quick look at the headlines reveals there is no peace in God's creation. A few years ago, I went to the library and looked at the headlines from a hundred years earlier. I was not terribly surprised to find the paper read like something that could have been written today: international conflicts between great powers; turmoil in the Middle East; economic inequity and uncertainty; and, locally, rampant crime. The situations were different, but the conflicts were eerily the same. Some things never change—or so it seems.

That, however, is not how God sees his creation. He wants better for us: he wants safety, life, love, peace. Is that a pipe dream? Quixotic? And if it is not, why hasn't the Lord intervened to rescue the innocent and save the weak who always suffer disproportionally? When is the Lion of Judah coming to usher in the time when "they will neither harm nor destroy on all my holy mountain"?

That's what we wait for, isn't it? Jesus came to destroy evil, sickness, and death itself. The message of the cross is that the victory is won. His resurrection is the promise of the Father that His faithful people, too, will rise and live in the restored creation that Jesus came to rescue. There is, however, more work to be done. In the time between the Lord's first and second coming we are to wait, watch, and act in such a manner that the vision of the Lord for His creation will be more and more realized.

In the parable of the wise and foolish virgins, Jesus tells us that we must be prepared to light the way for His return with acts of righteousness: acts that reflect the light of God. In a world of greed and selfishness, we are to live lives of self-giving and service. In a violent world, we are to be peacemakers, and in an unjust society, we are to honor truth and justice. We are not to wait passively, rather, we must be light in the world through our commitment to being the presence of Christ in our world until he comes again in glory.

Prayer

Father, You promise a day when the earth will be filled with knowledge of Your goodness, justice, and love. On that day, there will be an end to war, suffering, and death. All nature will be at peace, wolves and lambs will lie down safely, and there will be no violence, or killing in all Your creation. That day will come with the reign of the Lion of Judah who is the Lamb of God upon whom Your Spirit rests and through whom Your Spirit will come and fill all Your creation. Hasten that day; bring on that time.

Activity

In a note or card tell someone you love, that you love them.

#

Notes

Monday of the Fourth Week of Advent

Scripture

Sing, Daughter Zion;
shout aloud, Israel!
Be glad and rejoice with all your heart,
Daughter Jerusalem!
The Lord has taken away your punishment,
He has turned back your enemy.
The Lord, the King of Israel, is with you;
never again will you fear any harm.
On that day
they will say to Jerusalem,
'Do not fear, Zion;
do not let your hands hang limp.
The Lord your God is with you,
the Mighty Warrior who saves.
He will take great delight in you;
in his love, he will no longer rebuke you,
but will rejoice over you with singing'" (Zephaniah 3:14–17).

Reflection

In the first chapter of Zephaniah's short book, the prophet predicted the Lord's judgment would fall upon His faithless people. Judah sinned by worshiping idols, ignoring the poor and marginalized, and living as if God didn't exist or didn't matter. Our God, the God of Israel, will not be mocked!

Make no mistake about it: God takes action. He did so in ancient Israel, and He does so today. Yahweh will not tolerate faithlessness. He will punish people and nations that sin against Him. In the case of faithless Judah, the punishment would be swift and severe.

Zephaniah sees the trouble coming: Judah will be invaded and conquered by the Babylonian Empire, the reigning superpower of the day. Many Jews would lose their lives, and many more would suffer when their conquerors took the survivors as captives to Babylon, where they would be enslaved to their conquerors and where their offspring would remain in exile for seventy years.

God never punishes just to punish; however, He punishes so we might learn from our wayward ways and return to Him. Implicit, and often explicit, in God's punishment is a call to come back to Him. Repent, change your hearts, come home to Me, and let Me love you: all will be forgiven. Forsake your foolish and arrogant ways, the Lord seems to say. If you come to the Lord with humility and meekness, He will welcome you and restore your nation.

The last word from God is always *love*. Love in infinite abundance; love with no strings attached.

In the closing words of Zephaniah's book, he not only predicts the end of exile and the return of a faithful remnant to Judah, but he also foresees the time when God will end all the suffering that sin and faithlessness have caused.

The day is coming, he proclaims, when God's people will sing, rejoice, and be glad because God will take away the judgment (in Hebrew *mis·pat*, which refers to a legal judgment) against them because of their sinfulness. They will be acquitted of the burden of their sin, not due to their own merit but because of the gracious generosity of the Lord.

God will again dwell with His people, as He dwelt with Adam in the beginning. He will be Lord of all, removing danger and fear.

Have courage, be strong, the prophet says, because "the Lord is with you." Zephaniah anticipates Paul, who wrote to the Romans, "If God is for us, who can be against us?" (Romans 8:31b).

This prophecy is fulfilled in the coming of the Messiah. In Jesus' birth, life, and ministry, and in the saving events of His passion, death, and resurrection, God dwelt among us and saved us from sin and death forever. God, holding nothing back, put off His divinity to take upon Himself our humanity so He could save us by pouring out His love completely.

Paul continues reassuringly in the eighth chapter of His letter to the Romans:

"He who did not spare his own Son, but gave him up for us all—how will he not also, along with him, graciously give us all things? Who will bring any charge against those whom God has chosen? It is God who justifies. Who then is the one who condemns? No one. Christ Jesus who died—more than that, who was raised to life—is at the right hand of God and is also interceding for us. Who shall separate us from the love of Christ? Shall trouble or hardship or persecution or famine or nakedness or danger or sword? As it is written:

"For your sake, we face death all day long;
we are considered as sheep to be slaughtered"

No, in all these things we are more than conquerors through Him who loved us. For I am convinced that neither death nor life, neither angels nor demons, neither the present nor the future, nor any powers, neither height nor depth nor anything else in all creation, will be able to separate us from the love of God that is in Christ Jesus our Lord" (Romans 8:32–39).

In our faithless age, when we have, like the Jews of Zephaniah's day, also become a selfish, godless people, these remain comforting words: the Lord has come to save us, not to condemn.

His birth in Bethlehem began a saving mission that continues today. Jesus *is* Emmanuel; He is God with us! In the worst of times, we can rejoice in the Lord, as He rejoices in His beloved people.

Turn to Him and live.

Prayer

As you came to us once as a babe in Bethlehem, come again to us, complete Your victory over the forces of sin and death that seem so powerful. In times that can be so frightening, help us know that You are still with us. Your Spirit abides with us and will never leave us. We can have confidence that you are the Lord of history, and we have nothing to fear. Keep us faithful through the challenges of this life so we might find the fullness of life with you forever. We ask this in your Holy Name and through the Spirit, with the Father you are One God forever and ever. Amen,

Activity

Pray the prayer of the heart today (the prayer is commonly also called the *Jesus Prayer*). It is a mantra and works like this: Close your eyes as you sit up straight in a comfortable chair, but not too comfortable. Take a deep breath in, and as you do so, pray the words "Lord Jesus Christ, Son of the Living God." Pause a moment, then breathe out, completing the prayer with the words "Have mercy on me, a sinner." Repeat this prayer at least a hundred times, remembering to yoke the words with your breath. While not fighting distractions, should they occur, try to focus on the words and on your breath. This prayer, which comes to us from the Russian Church, is a precious gift and has brought many closer to the Lord. Do this every day from now to at least the end of the Christmas season on the feast of the Epiphany (January 6th).

#

Notes

Tuesday of the Fourth Week of Advent

Scripture
"In the sixth month of Elizabeth's pregnancy, God sent the angel Gabriel to Nazareth, a town in Galilee, to a virgin pledged to be married to a man named Joseph, a descendant of David. The virgin's name was Mary. The angel went to her and said, 'Greetings, you who are highly favored! The Lord is with you.'

Mary was greatly troubled by his words and wondered what kind of greeting this might be. But the angel said to her, 'Do not be afraid, Mary; you have found favor with God. You will conceive and give birth to a son, and you are to call him Jesus. He will be great and will be called the Son of the Most High. The Lord God will give him the throne of his father David, and he will reign over Jacob's descendants forever; his kingdom will never end.'

'How will this be,' Mary asked the angel, 'since I am a virgin?'

The angel answered, 'The Holy Spirit will come on you, and the power of the Most High will overshadow you. So the holy one to be born will be called the Son of God. Even Elizabeth, your relative is going to have a child in her old age, and she who was said to be unable to conceive is in her sixth month. For no word from God will ever fail.'

'I am the Lord's servant,' Mary answered. 'May your word to me be fulfilled.' Then the angel left her" (Luke 1:26–38).

Reflection
The visit of the angel Gabriel and his message to Mary would change not only her life but also the entire arc of human history.

When Gabriel appeared to Mary, who was little more than a child, she must have felt a combination of awe and dread. Gabriel went right to the heart of his mission and greeted Mary, saying, "Be filled with joy and rejoicing, Mary." This will be good news—and the angel makes this clear from the start.

God's messenger explains that Mary has been gifted with grace, with God's favor and love. This is purely an act of God, not in any way due to Mary's merit. The God of Israel is a God of election - he chooses as he chooses: He chooses the weak and powerless to accomplish his will. Now, he calls an illiterate teenage girl to be the vessel through which the Logos would take on flesh and walk among us.

Mary was "troubled" at the angel's words (Luke 1:29). This might be the greatest of all biblical understatements. Mary was likely terrified, unsure of what the angel's message meant for her, for her life, for her plans, and her upcoming marriage. Gabriel counseled her: "Do not be afraid, Mary, for you have found favor with God" (Luke 1:30). We are not told how well this assurance calmed Mary's fears, but she continued to listen to Gabriel and ponder the message he brought.

The angel's next revelation must have caused Mary's heart to skip a beat and her mind to raise new questions about the mysterious ways of the God of Israel: "And behold you will conceive in your womb and bear a son and shall call His name Jesus" (Luke 1:31). God promised a new Adam who would reverse the disobedience of our first parents and restore humanity to its prelapsarian perfection (Genesis 3:15). Mary was to be the mother of the long-awaited Messiah, the great King who would sit on David's throne, and reign over the house of Jacob forever (Luke 1:32-33).

Mary's faith was strong, but she needed to know some particulars. To Mary, the young virgin who cherished God's law and who was betrothed to Joseph, this announcement must have come as a stunning surprise. Mary did not doubt the angel, but she knew enough about the way babies are conceived to know she couldn't be pregnant because of her virginity.

The power of the Spirit of God, the Ruach Yahweh (literally the "Breath of God") would come upon her so her child would be not only her son but also the son of God (Luke 1:35b). God was moving in the world and among his people.

"Then Mary said, 'Behold the maidservant of the Lord1 Let it be to me according to your word'" (Luke 1:38a). More plainly put, Mary said yes to God, despite her uncertainty and questions. God's plan to rescue his beloved creation from sin and death would be implemented. The final act of God's plan of salvation began with Mary's yes. The faithfulness of a teenager in a remote part of the Roman Empire thousands of years ago made our salvation possible. The world would know Immanuel because Mary first welcomed the son of God to be with her in the temple of her body.

Prayer
Saving Lord, we are blessed by the example of Your mother. Though only a child herself, she welcomed You into the temple of her body and into the world You came to save. By carrying You into the world, she becomes the image of your church, for we are also called to carry Your presence in the world. As she welcomed you into her body, so may we welcome Your Holy Spirit. May our bodies be His temple. May everything we do give witness to our love of You and for the least of our brothers and sisters. We ask this of the Father in Your name, and through the Spirit's power, You are One God forever and ever. Amen.

Activity

Find some way to give concrete witness to the power and presence of Christ in your life. How has God been present to you or in you? Share that story with someone else; that story has God's power in it. Do something this Christmas season for those who may be lonely or sad. Do you have an elderly relative or neighbor who might be lonely? Visit them; maybe you'd like to invite them to share Christmas dinner with you.

\#

Notes

122

Wednesday of the Fourth Week of Advent#

Scripture
"This is how the birth of Jesus the Messiah came about: His mother Mary was pledged to be married to Joseph, but before they came together, she was found to be pregnant through the Holy Spirit. Because Joseph, her husband was faithful to the law, and yet did not want to expose her to public disgrace, he had in mind to divorce her quietly.

But after he had considered this, an angel of the Lord appeared to him in a dream and said, 'Joseph son of David, do not be afraid to take Mary home as your wife because what is conceived in her is from the Holy Spirit. She will give birth to a son, and you are to give him the name Jesus because he will save his people from their sins.'

All this took place to fulfill what the Lord had said through the prophet: 'The virgin will conceive and give birth to a son, and they will call him Immanuel (which means 'God with us')'" (Matthew 1:18–23).

Reflection
Mary was unwed, pregnant, and had no better explanation for her condition than that "she was... with child of the Holy Spirit" (Matt. 1:18b). How do you think Mary's parents took that news? How would that explanation work with you if your fiancée was going to have a baby and you knew you were not the father? While we know Mary was, in fact, with child of the Holy Spirit, most, if not all, of her family and friends would think of her as a sinner, an adulteress. Under the law of Moses, the penalty for adultery was death by stoning. If not executed, and it is highly unlikely she would have been since Roman law would not have

permitted it, she certainly would have been shunned and treated as a pariah by the people of Nazareth.

Joseph didn't buy the "Holy Spirit" explanation. He felt betrayed and hurt, as any man in a similar situation would have felt. Joseph was a decent and kind man, though, and because of her perceived unfaithfulness, he didn't want to marry Mary, but he didn't want to destroy her either. "Joseph, her husband, was faithful to the law, and yet did not want to expose her to public disgrace, he had in mind to put her away quietly" (Matthew 1:19). "Let's handle this quietly," Joseph reasoned. "People don't have to know, but neither should I marry a woman I can't trust and who has been unfaithful to me."

Again, it is an angel that reveals the hidden plan of God. An angel of the Lord appeared to him in a dream and said, "Joseph, son of David, do not be afraid to take Mary home as your wife because what is conceived in her is from the Holy Spirit. She will give birth to a son, and you are to give him the name Jesus because he will save his people from their sins" (Matthew 1:20–21).

Joseph is a dreamer, like the earlier Joseph, son of Jacob. He knew God often speaks to us through our dreams and imagination. He trusted the angel who brought him a surprising and hopeful message. Mary had told the truth! The Holy Spirit did come over her, and the child in her womb would be the Messiah, the Son of God.

Trusting God, Joseph could now trust Mary. Joseph would be a protecting and guiding presence in the critical years surrounding Jesus' birth and childhood. By taking Mary as his wife, Joseph shielded her from the scorn of their neighbors. Mary's reputation would remain intact as she bore her first child. Cooperating with the Spirit himself, Joseph would not have marital relations with Mary until the child was born. Then, faithful to the angel's command, Joseph named Mary's child Jesus. From the moment of Jesus' conception, God was with us as He had never been before.

Prayer

Lord Jesus, in Your birth, You embodied the presence of God in the world. Your mother, only a child herself, welcomed You and carried You into the world as an infant. Like her, we have been called to be Christ-bearers. Help us to be faithful to that calling and bring Your Holy Spirit to the world through our loving kindness and faithfulness to Your gospel and Your truth. As your mother was obedient to the Father, so may we be in every moment of our lives. We ask this in Your Holy Name; You are the one who came to be Emmanuel, God with us. With the Father and the Spirit, You are One God forever. Amen.

Activity

Sometimes, the Lord asks us to do things we don't quite understand, and He asks us to trust him. Joseph is an example of this trusting obedience, as is Mary, whom we are told held in her heart many things she didn't quite understand about her firstborn. Perhaps there is something in your life you don't understand: maybe a child who seems to be going off course or a loved one whose choices you might disapprove of. It could be something at work that bothers you: the behavior of a co-worker or the decisions of the boss. Whatever it is, you have a choice: you can decide how to respond to the person or situation. You can be judgmental, or you can withhold judgment and give the benefit of the doubt. You can certainly pray for guidance, wisdom, and understanding. So, today, reflect on the things in your life that may confuse or bother you. Take them to God in prayer and follow the guidance you are given. Just as He spoke to Joseph, He will speak to you. Listen!

#

Notes

Thursday of the Fourth Week of Advent

Scripture

"This is what Isaiah son of Amoz saw concerning Judah and Jerusalem:

In the last days, the mountain of the Lord's temple will be established
as the highest of the mountains;
it will be exalted above the hills,
and all nations will stream to it.

Many peoples will come and say,
'Come, let us go up to the mountain of the Lord,
to the temple of the God of Jacob.
He will teach us his ways,
so that we may walk in his paths.'
The law will go out from Zion,
the word of the Lord from Jerusalem.

He will judge between the nations
and will settle disputes for many peoples.
They will beat their swords into plowshares
and their spears into pruning hooks.
Nation will not take up sword against nation,
nor will they train for war anymore.

Come, descendants of Jacob,
let us walk in the light of the Lord" (Isaiah 2:1–5).

Reflection

Israel's God, Yahweh, is not like a clockmaker who sets creation in motion but does nothing more. He cares about His creation and is active in history. But if that is true, why is the world such a mess? Why does evil among us continue to prosper and thrive (or so it seems)? Why do good people suffer? Why are there wars in which we see wanton destruction and death? Why are children, the most innocent among us, brutalized and killed before they have a chance to live?

If God acts in history, why isn't He doing a better job?

Archibald MacLeish's character, J.B, in the play by the same name, states the dilemma succinctly: "If God is God, he is not good. If God is good, he is not God."

The Jewish prophets take a longer view: God has eternity to win His victory, but he *will* win.

Isaiah writes about his vision of "the last days" when history is fulfilled. It will be a time when God Himself will judge, and He will judge fairly and end all disputes equitably. He will teach not only the Jews but all people to walk in His way of love and compassion. He will set all injustices right and end all suffering. Wars will no longer occur because God's peace and love will prevail throughout the earth. In the fullness of time, Israel's Yahweh will prove himself to be both God and good!

In Jesus, the end time begins—one might say that Jesus' life and death lived in obedience to the Father won the victory over sin and death forever. Jesus inaugurates the beginning of the end times. God's victory will be complete when He returns at the end of days. Then, in the radiance of the new heaven and the new earth promised in the book of Revelation, all nations will know there is no God but the God of Israel, and they will "stream" to God's holy mountain, Jerusalem.

Prayer

Lord Jesus, You are the obedient Son of the Father. You show us that obedience to God is the only path leading to life. Open our minds and hearts to the Spirit within us who shows us the way. The Spirit is our guide and advocate, our helper and friend. Make us completely obedient to the urgings of the Spirit. Give us discernment to know the Spirit's voice from the many other counterfeit voices that tug at us. May we only serve You, and may we be faithful to You all the days of our lives.

\

Activity

Isaiah wrote of a faithful God to a faithless nation. Our own nation, once proud to pledge itself to be "under God," has strayed far from that aspiration. Our currency contains the motto "In God we trust," though we trust more in money and the power and security it seems to provide than we trust in God, who is our only real help in times of trouble. So today, take some time to commit yourself to God as your only hope. Then, reaffirm that you place your trust in Him *alone*, not in politicians, celebrities, or finances. Finally, pray for the nation. Ask the Lord to send godly leaders who will do what is right, restore equal justice under our laws, and protect the powerless among us.

#

Notes

Friday of the Fourth Week of Advent

Scripture

"Now, there was a man in Jerusalem called Simeon, who was righteous and devout. He was waiting for the consolation of Israel, and the Holy Spirit was on him. It had been revealed to him by the Holy Spirit that he would not die before he had seen the Lord's Messiah. Moved by the Spirit, he went into the temple courts. When the parents brought in the child Jesus to do for him what the custom of the Law required, Simeon took him in his arms and praised God, saying:

'Sovereign Lord, as you have promised,
you may now dismiss your servant in peace.
  For my eyes have seen your salvation,
    which you have prepared in the sight of all nations:
    a light for revelation to the Gentiles,
and the glory of your people Israel.'

The child's father and mother marveled at what was said about him" (Luke 2:25–33).

Reflection

What do we know about Simeon from this short passage in Luke's gospel? Quite a bit, really.

First, we know he was a good Jew: a righteous man whose spirit was formed by the Torah. Simeon strove to faithfully obey God's statutes and precepts, day in and day out.

Second, Simeon was *devoted* to the God of Abraham. His religious practice was not simply a wooden outward observance of the type Jesus would later condemn in the Pharisees:

"These people honor me with their lips,
but their hearts are far from me.
They worship me in vain;
their teachings are merely human rules" (Matthew 15:8–9).

No, Simeon's life was a testament to his heartfelt trust in the Lord's promises. He did not just believe in God's Word; it shaped his very being and guided his actions. This man loved and trusted God with unwavering faith.

The third thing we learn about Simeon is that he patiently waited for the Lord to fulfill His promises and keep His word. Time passed, but Simeon never wavered in his belief that God is as good as His word.

Finally, the Holy Spirit was upon Simeon. Simeon was a deeply prayerful man who listened to God's Spirit within him. The Spirit sometimes speaks with the roar of thunder but more often comes to us in the stillness and quiet of a listening heart. When Simeon heard the Spirit speak within him, he believed and acted. When the Lord told Simeon he would live to see Israel's consolation, he believed, watched, and waited. When the Lord told Simeon to go up to the temple, he went up with expectation. When, on that day, he saw a poor couple with their first child, he knew this child was the one for whom he, Israel, and indeed the whole world, waited.

Simeon was a man of Advent. We find him waiting at dawn, after a long night of darkness, for the break of the day.

His story invites us to be like him in righteousness, devotion, and trust. He challenges us to strive to do God's will daily in the sometimes-dreary monotony of our lives as we wait for the One-Who-Came to come anew. And come He does; we can see His presence every day as we wait for His coming at the end of days.

As the years turn into centuries and millennia, it is easy to forget the promise: "This same Jesus, who has been taken from you into heaven, will come back in the same way you have seen him go into heaven" (Acts 1:11). Simeon's story challenges us to wait patiently and with confidence, trusting that God's promises—all of them—will be kept at just the right time and just the right way.

While we wait for the Lord, our striving must include an embrace of Scripture and prayer that invites God's Holy Spirit to come upon us and guide us. We must take time for prayer every day. We need to be in the Word; daily Bible reading is imperative. How are we to know of God's promises and his love if we don't read the Word? Finally, by taking time every day to sit quietly in prayerful meditation, we can train our hearts and minds to listen to the Spirit amid the noise of our clattering world.

Prayer

Creator God, give us Advent hearts. Send Your Spirit upon us and open our hearts and minds to the Spirit's inspiration. Make us, like Simeon, men and women who strive to live lives devoted to You through prayer, the study of Scripture, and the showing of kindness. Give us eyes to see Your presence and action in our lives and create patient and trustful hearts that believe Your promises and wait for the day when the Lord returns, and Your will to be done on earth as it is in Heaven. We ask this in the holy name of Jesus and through the power of the Spirit, with You they are One God forever and ever. Amen.

Activity

Spend time in silent meditation, listening for the voice of the Spirit within you. Sit in a comfortable, but not too comfortable, chair (you don't want to fall asleep). Close your eyes or light a candle and focus your gaze on the candle's flame. Pick some sacred word or phrase such as "Abba," "Holy Spirit, come," or "Yahweh." Then, focus on the word as you breathe in and out. Breathing in, say your sacred word, breathing out, say it again, or complete the phrase. You can expect to be distracted by the chatter in your mind; that is normal and nothing to be concerned about. Don't fight whatever thought distracts you; return your focus to your breath and your sacred word. Do this for as long as you like. Those new to meditation should start with only ten minutes but go longer if you're accustomed to meditating.

#

Notes

135

Christmas Eve

Scripture

"In those days Caesar Augustus issued a decree that a census should be taken of the entire Roman world. (This was the first census that took place while Quirinius was governor of Syria.) And everyone went to their own town to register.

So Joseph also went up from the town of Nazareth in Galilee to Judea, to Bethlehem the town of David because he belonged to the house and line of David. He went there to register with Mary, who was pledged to be married to him and was expecting a child. While they were there, the time came for the baby to be born, and she gave birth to her firstborn, a son. She wrapped him in cloths and placed him in a manger because there was no guest room available for them" (Luke 2:1–7).

Reflection

They couldn't be more different! Augustus Caesar and Jesus!

Jesus, the child of Jewish peasants, was born in Bethlehem, a small town in a backwater province of the Roman Empire. He was delivered in a stable with a manger his first crib. There was nothing portentous about His birth, nothing to suggest greatness. He would grow up to work with his hands, He proclaimed the nearness of the reign of God in his ministry, and he was executed on a Roman cross; a more insignificant life could hardly be imagined.

Augustus, on the other hand, was the child of privilege, adopted by Julius Caesar as a youth. He would succeed his father as ruler of a vast empire. He lived in a palace, enjoyed great luxury from the moment of his birth, and reigned over his dominions for almost sixty years, he was the most powerful man on earth. He ushered in the *Pax Romana* (the peace of Rome), a time of unprecedented peace and prosperity throughout the world. It would last more than two hundred years. Ironically, it is not Augustus but the insignificant child of Mary who would be known forever as the "Prince of Peace."

Jesus' birth was not easy, not for Mary, not for Joseph. While from Nazareth in Galilee, the young couple was required by Augustus' decree to travel to Bethlehem and register for a census; it was a ninety-mile trip and not an easy one. Once they arrived in Bethlehem, they could find no lodging and were required to take shelter in a stable, and it was here Jesus was born and laid in a bed made for him in a manger.

Few observed this birth, which would shake the Roman Empire to its core in a few short years and ultimately change the arc of world history. Some shepherds came, having heard angels singing God's glory over the birth of a child in Bethlehem, and three foreigners came from a distant land bringing gifts to "the newborn King," but few others took notice.

The witnesses to Jesus' birth are those he would later call blessed: the poor, the marginalized, and the vulnerable. Few in Bethlehem recognized Jesus as who he was; for most, he was considered a poor child of a poor Jewish peasant couple, nothing special. It took faith and a chorus of angels to get a handful of shepherds who were out on the hillsides tending their sheep to begin to understand that God was, in and through this child, moving powerfully among his people to rescue all of humankind from sin and death.

We often fail to hear those herald angels singing today, yet they do sing on. They invite us to see God's presence and power moving in the world still, in his beloved little ones. They call us to recognize Jesus in the face of the sick, the elderly, the lonely, and the poor. That is where we can meet the Lord face to face today.

> How silently, how silently
> The wondrous Gift is given!
> So God imparts to human hearts
> The blessings of His heaven
> No ear may hear His coming
> But in this world of sin
> Where meek souls will receive Him still
> The dear Christ enters in.
> "O Little Town of Bethlehem" vs. 3

Prayer
Faithful God, Your Son was born in humble circumstances. His first crib was a feeding trough in a stable, yet in that child, all of history hung in the balance. In Jesus, divinity entered humanity to rescue and save Your people from sin and death. As we reflect on His coming to us as a humble child in Bethlehem, do not let us forget that He will come again in the light of Your glory, and when He comes, He will rescue your entire creation, wipe the tears from all eyes, and usher in the new heaven and new earth. Bring on the day, Lord, and hasten the time. Amen.

Activity

Many children today are born in humble circumstances; their families are poor, sometimes too poor to even afford Christmas presents. We can help them. The Marine Corps collects "Toys for Tots" every year, and there are organizations like that in every community. Find some way to make Christmas better for a family in need. If you can't donate toys or food, give of your time and volunteer.

#

Notes

141

Christmas Day

Scripture

"And there were shepherds living out in the fields nearby, keeping watch over their flocks at night. An angel of the Lord appeared to them, and the glory of the Lord shone around them, and they were terrified. But the angel said to them, 'Do not be afraid. I bring you good news that will cause great joy for all the people. Today, in the town of David, a Savior has been born to you; he is the Messiah, the Lord. This will be a sign to you: You will find a baby wrapped in cloths and lying in a manger.'

Suddenly a great company of the heavenly host appeared with the angel, praising God and saying,

'Glory to God in the highest heaven,
and on earth peace to those on whom his favor rests.'

When the angels had left them and gone into heaven, the shepherds said to one another, 'Let's go to Bethlehem and see this thing that has happened, which the Lord has told us about'" (Luke 2:8–15).

Reflection

God has never studied marketing, and it shows!

Had the Lord consulted the wizards of smart marketing on Madison Avenue, they would have told Him the best way to get the word out about the birth of the Messiah would be to get the word out to the important people, the folks who really mattered. "Start with the Emperor," they might say. "There is no better way to get the news of the holy birth out to the entire world than to capture the attention of Caesar. Other important folks should also be apprised of your action, Lord." They would go on: "After all, this is the birth of the Jewish Messiah, so Jewish elites should also be high on the list of folks to get the message: the High Priest, the Torah scholars, an important Pharisee or two, and of course the local Roman vassal, Herod. Next, there must be wealthy people and local celebrities in and around Bethlehem; get them on board. You will have a winner of a publicity campaign if you do all that."

Luckily, God didn't consult marketing executives. He announced the birth of Jesus His way. "For the foolishness of God is wiser than human wisdom, and the weakness of God is stronger than human strength" (1 Corinthians 25).

He sent his angels to proclaim the good news of the Messiah's birth to the most unlikely audience: shepherds grazing their flocks at night. Shepherds were at the bottom of the social heap at the time of Jesus' birth. Their pay was terrible, their hours long, and they worked with sheep! Sheep may be cute, but they're not the smartest things on four legs and cannot even defend themselves from predators. It was hard, thankless, humbling work: not many Jewish mothers of the time hoped their kids would grow up to be shepherds.

Yet to these lowly men protecting their sheep at night in the hills outside Bethlehem, the Lord first revealed the birth of our Lord. "Today, in the town of David, a Savior has been born to you; he is the Messiah." the angels announced. The long-awaited One had finally come, and God sent his messengers *not* to the great, famous, or well-connected. He sent those herald angels to poor, insignificant, marginalized men. He chooses the weak and small of this world to confound the proud. He did it then, He continues to do it today.

The sign the angels gave the shepherds was equally curious: "You will find a baby wrapped in cloths and lying in a manger." Not very impressive when you think about it: a poor baby lying in a feeding trough. Yet in that child, "the hopes and fears of all the years" are met. Someone more sophisticated or cynical might have thought that a child in the manger was no big deal; not these shepherds! They went to Bethlehem, found Mary, Joseph, and the infant Jesus, and they were amazed. They believed the good news and shared it as good evangelists should. Luke tells us the shepherds went home sharing what the angels told them and what they saw.

The Christmas message is good news to the poor, and aren't we all poor as we stand before the Mighty One? The humble need God's message of hope and peace and welcome it when they hear it; only when we realize how lost and broken, we are do we understand our need for salvation. The shepherds' hearts longed for the angelic message, and that's why they were a perfect group to tell the Christmas message. They went home believing God had begun a great thing and praising God with joy in their hearts.

For the most part, over twenty centuries, all the emperors, kings, high priests, and lawyers have made little impact on the world, and have been mostly forgotten. So have the shepherds, for that matter. That child in the manger, however, continues to inspire, transform, and save the suffering and poor of every generation. May our hearts and minds be open to him as he is born in us again every day.

> O Holy Child of Bethlehem
> Descend to us, we pray
> Cast out our sin and enter in
> Be born in us today

We hear the Christmas angels
The great glad tidings tell
O come to us, abide with us
Our Lord Emmanuel.

"O Little Town of Bethlehem" vs. 4

Prayer

Creator God, You had the birth of Your Son Jesus announced to humble shepherds protecting their flocks; they heard the angels' announcement and believed the good news they proclaimed of the Savior's birth. We, too, have heard the good news proclaimed to us. Deepen our belief in the transforming power of Jesus to bring us joy on earth and eternal life with You in Your Kingdom. We ask this in Jesus' name and through the Spirit. They are One God with You forever. Amen.

Activity

The message of our Savior, first proclaimed to shepherds on a hillside near Bethlehem, must be proclaimed to the ends of the earth. People come to faith by hearing the good news shared by believers. *Every* Christian has a story of faith to share, a story that has power. What transformed you can inspire countless others. Think about how you have experienced God's power in your life. Share that story with a family member, friend, or acquaintance who may need to hear it.

\#

Notes

147

Second Day of Christmas - the Feast of Stephen

Scripture

"Stephen, full of the Holy Spirit, looked up to heaven and saw the glory of God, and Jesus standing at the right hand of God. 'Look,' he said, 'I see heaven open and the Son of Man standing at the right hand of God.' At this they covered their ears and, yelling at the top of their voices, they all rushed at him, dragged him out of the city, and began to stone him. Meanwhile, the witnesses laid their coats at the feet of a young man named Saul.

While they were stoning him, Stephen prayed, 'Lord Jesus, receive my spirit.' Then he fell on his knees and cried out, 'Lord, do not hold this sin against them.' When he had said this, he fell asleep" (Acts 7:55–60).

Reflection

"No man has greater love than this than to lay down his life for his friends" (John 15:13, my translation). On the cross, Jesus laid down His life for Stephen and all of us. Stephen shows his love and appreciation for Jesus' sacrifice by willingly offering his life as a witness to his faith in the Lord. Called the protomartyr, Stephen is the first of many throughout history to choose death rather than deny their crucified and risen Lord.

There are many similarities between the deaths of Stephen and Jesus'. Like Jesus, Stephen was falsely accused of blasphemy by those who "could not stand up against the wisdom the Spirit gave him as he spoke" (Acts 6:10). As Jesus' antagonists stirred up the crowd to demand the Lord's crucifixion, so also Stephen's adversaries agitated a mob with false claims that Stephen blasphemed against Moses and God. Jesus was put to death outside the walls of Jerusalem, and like Him, Stephen's murderous mob dragged him outside the city walls and stoned him to death.

To the end, Stephen remained faithful to his Savior. Stephen was filled with the Lord's Spirit even as he was dragged to his execution. Echoing Jesus' forgiving words from the cross, Stephen prayed for the very people who killed him. Among the objects of that prayer was Saul, a young Pharisee at whose feet Stephen's murderers had laid their garments. Saul became an ardent persecutor of the Christians in Jerusalem and throughout the region. The prayers of the righteous have power, though. The same Saul would become Paul, the single greatest promotor of the gospel of the Lord, perhaps of all time. Stephen's story takes up a little more than a chapter in Acts; Paul's letters will continue to inspire Christians forever.

In Paul, Stephen's prayer for his persecutors was answered.

Prayer

Forgiving Lord, Your power to transform knows no bounds. There is no situation beyond Your power to redeem. You work all things together for the good of Your beloved children. Your servant Stephen showed compassion for his persecutors. Like him, please give us a forgiving and compassionate heart. We believe You hear our prayers and sometimes answer us in surprising and miraculous ways. Open our eyes to see Your presence all around us and within us. We ask this in the powerful name of Jesus. Amen.

Activity

This is the Christmas season, a time of joy and giving. Christians give gifts to each other during this time in remembrance of the great gift of the Incarnation: God Himself took on our humanity so we might become His children.

Stephen's faith in Christ gave the gift of the gospel to all who would hear him. Perhaps Saul, presiding over his execution, was moved by something Stephen said or did in his final moments. To know Christ is to receive the gift of life itself.

Find some way to share your faith with another: a family member, perhaps, or a neighbor, or even someone you meet in the course of your day. God will lead you to the right person and give you the wisdom to know what to say and how to say it. Ask the Lord for that gift. Start this and all things with prayer.

Stephen also gave the gift of forgiveness. In any life lived with others, we will be hurt or offended—sometimes inadvertently and others on purpose. The motive doesn't matter; what matters is that we give the gift of forgiveness as Stephen did. Notice how Stephan forgave: he prayed for his murderers and let go of all animosity.

Today, let go of anything you hold against others in your heart. Do it intentionally. You don't have to tell anyone; just acknowledge it in your heart and thereby set yourself free. The best, and perhaps only, way to do that is by praying for those people who get under your skin. Ask God to bless and care for them and ask Him to give you compassion from His Holy Spirit.

Here's one last thing you might do to ritualize your forgiveness: on slips of paper, write down the grudges and complaints you are releasing, put the slips into a bowl of some sort, take them outside, and burn them. Watch the smoke take your burdens away and give thanks for the gift God has given you, the gift of being able to forgive, and the gift of inner peace.

#

Notes

152

The Third Day of Christmas

Scripture

"That which was from the beginning, which we have heard, which we have seen with our eyes, which we have looked at and our hands have touched—this we proclaim concerning the Word of life. The life appeared; we have seen it and testify to it, and we proclaim to you the eternal life, which was with the Father and has appeared to us. We proclaim to you what we have seen and heard, so that you also may have fellowship with us. And our fellowship is with the Father and with his Son, Jesus Christ. We write this to make our joy complete" (1 John 1:1–4).

Reflection

One snowy winter day in the first decade of the eleventh century, Francis of Assisi walked home from Perugia, a distance of almost fourteen miles, with his frequent companion, Brother Leo. As they walked, Francis mused about perfect joy. Joy is not found, Francis told Leo, in success, even spiritual success. Nor can joy be found in fame and recognition. Francis believed perfect joy could only be found by patiently enduring injustice and suffering as Christ had patiently endured the cross. Living in fellowship with Jesus is a perfect joy.

Christmas celebrates the eternal Word of God (the Logos) becoming human. John is an eyewitness to Jesus' ministry and resurrection: he saw the Lord with his eyes, touched Him, and experienced Him giving the blind sight and raising the dead. John was there to listen to the Sermon on the Mount. Love, Jesus taught, is the greatest commandment of the Law; John was there to marvel at Jesus' wisdom when He spoke those words: Love the Lord your God with all that is in you and love your neighbor as yourself.

John's heart was broken that dark Friday when Jesus was crucified, and his sadness was turned to joy when, on the third day, Jesus rose from the grave, as He had promised, putting an end to death forever. In the upper room, fifty days later, John heard the rushing wind and felt the fire of the Holy Spirit, the Advocate sent by Jesus to guide and inspire us until the end of the ages.

John knows whereof he speaks: Jesus is Lord of life. He was one with the Father at the dawn of time; all things were created through Him and for Him. In becoming human, He redeemed sinful humanity and saved us from death because our God is the author of life. Eternal life is now ours, a gift of God in Christ.

God wants us to live with Him eternally, as Jesus says in His high-priestly prayer. Addressed to the Father, Jesus prays: "[T]he hour has come. Glorify your Son, that your Son may glorify you, for you granted him authority over all people that he might give eternal life to all those you have given him. Now this is eternal life: that they know you, the only true God, and Jesus Christ, whom you have sent" (John 17:1–3).

Knowing the Lord and living in fellowship with Him is perfect joy; it is to receive the gift of eternal life not in heaven but in the lives we are living right now.

Prayer
Lord Jesus, thank You for Your divine humility. When You became man in Your incarnation, You became fully human while remaining fully divine. Your humble origins bespeak the humble character of God. Your mother was a child whose purity reminds us of what You desire for all children. Born in a stable surrounded by shepherds, given a manger as a crib, You remind us of Your love for the lowly and humble of the world. When we encounter people who struggle and suffer, show us how to help and love them. Let

us see the world with Your eyes so that we might recognize the divine image in all our brothers and sisters, no matter how much sin may have tarnished that image. Deepen our knowledge of and presence to Your Father, the one True God. He sent You, His Son, to share our struggles, to be one with our suffering, and to give us eternal life. We ask all this in Your holy name and through the Spirit, with the Father You are One God. Amen.

Activity

Volunteer to help feed the guests at a soup kitchen or some other place where the hungry and homeless are fed: places like this can be found in every community. As you serve with other volunteers, pray for the people you serve. They will likely be different than you in language or ethnicity, but they share our common humanity. They were uniquely and lovingly created; like you, they bear the image of their Creator and of the Eternal Word through whom all things came into being and were made.

#

Notes

The Fourth Day of Christmas - the Holy Innocents

Scripture

"When they [the magi] had gone, an angel of the Lord appeared to Joseph in a dream. 'Get up,' he said, 'take the child and his mother and escape to Egypt. Stay there until I tell you, for Herod is going to search for the child to kill him.'

So he got up, took the child and his mother during the night, and left for Egypt, where he stayed until the death of Herod. And so was fulfilled what the Lord had said through the prophet: 'Out of Egypt, I called my son.'

When Herod realized that he had been outwitted by the Magi, he was furious, and he gave orders to kill all the boys in Bethlehem and its vicinity who were two years old and under, in accordance with the time he had learned from the Magi" (Matthew 2:13–16).

Reflection

Every aspect of this passage speaks about the mission the Child begins at Bethlehem.

The magi themselves tell us Jesus has come not just for the children of Abraham but for all nations. The magi are foreigners, after all. They come from a distant land to honor the King worthy of their worship. In Matthew's gospel, these visitors from the East remind us that the good news signaled by the star of Bethlehem is for all people of all time. It reminds us, too, that if we are to honor the Child with our gifts, the gifts are to be offered without regard to senseless distinctions of race, gender, or theory. God loves us all, despite the arbitrary distinctions with which we see the world, and our love must reflect His. No one, not even our enemies, should be beyond our compassionate concern.

Matthew portrays Jesus as having the same childhood struggles that afflicted Moses. In the opening passages of Exodus, the Egyptian pharaoh, fearing the power of the Hebrews in his country, commands midwives to kill every newborn male Hebrew infant by throwing the child into the Nile. Moses was saved from this fate by God's intervention and grew to be the liberator of God's people.

Like Moses, Jesus is the target of a paranoid king who ordered all boys under the age of two in Bethlehem and its environs to be killed simply to destroy the child sought by the magi, the one born to be King of the Jews. Divine intervention saves Jesus in the form of an angel sent to Joseph in a dream. Telling Joseph to take Mary and the child to Egypt for safety further connects Jesus' birth and Moses' story.

For us, this is a reminder that while Jesus' birth is good news for the nations (in Latin for the *gentes*, from which we get the word *gentile*), Jesus' mission *is* to be Israel's long-awaited Messiah. Jesus will fulfill God's promise to Abraham that "all peoples on earth will be blessed through you" (Genesis 12:3b). God's wisdom unites Jews and Gentiles. The good news is for us all and there is no room for division between people. As Paul later wrote: "There is neither Jew nor Gentile, neither slave nor free, nor is there male and female, for you are all one in Christ Jesus" (Galatians 3:28). Our challenge is to put all divisiveness and hatred aside and love as the Lord has loved us all.

Finally, the murder of the Holy Innocents reminds us, at the beginning of His life, that Jesus would be God's Suffering Servant.

The shadow of the cross looms over Jesus at His birth. Jesus' journey that began in Bethlehem ultimately led to Calvary: His complete surrender to the Father in loving, absolute self-gift.

If we are to follow Him, our journeys must be like His. He tells us as much: "Whoever wants to be my disciple must deny themselves, take up their cross, and follow me" (Matthew 16:24).

Prayer

Father God, Your Son Jesus is a light to all the nations. His love reaches the ends of the earth, and His compassion extends to every human being, no matter how battered and scarred by sin that person may appear to our eyes. In Your eyes, that same person is a beloved child, and the Good Shepherd seeks to find and save him. Help us have eyes and a heart like our Savior's: give us the grace to see others as You see them and to love them as You love them. Create a forgiving spirit in us and give us the generosity to put Your beloved children and Your will and righteousness ahead of our desires and plans. Your Son gave everything to save us, so also give us generous hearts willing to sacrifice for the sake of Your kingdom and Your beloved people. We ask all this in Jesus' holy name. He is, with You and the Holy Spirit, One God forever and ever. Amen.

Activity

The Holy Innocents were children who were ripped from their parent's arms and put to death by a heartless tyrant whose heart was full of evil and deceit. Unfortunately, in the more than two thousand years since the deaths of those precious children, evil people have not stopped the persecution and destruction of the most innocent among us.

Sadly, throughout the world today, the scourge of abortion snuffs out the lives of children before they have had a chance to live. The merchants of death in the abortion establishment make enormous profits not only on abortion procedures themselves but also in the sale of fetal body parts. Christians are silent, for the most part, fearing censure, ridicule, or worse.

Raise your voice and let it be heard: write to your local newspaper and speak out against the culture of death. More importantly, find a service in your community that helps young, frightened women who are pregnant to carry their children to term and then put them up for adoption. These women often need financial help, psychological intervention, and moral support. We who believe that every life is a gift from the Creator have a moral obligation to do something concrete to help these women through a difficult period and then get back on their feet.

#

Notes

The Fifth Day of Christmas

Scripture
"It is too small a thing for you to be my servant
to restore the tribes of Jacob
and bring back those of Israel I have kept.
I will also make you a light for the Gentiles,
that my salvation may reach to the ends of the earth" (Isaiah
49:6).

"When Jesus spoke again to the people, he said, 'I am the light
of the world. Whoever follows me will never walk in darkness but
will have the light of life'" (John 8:12).

"You are the light of the world. A town built on a hill cannot
be hidden. Neither do people light a lamp and put it under a bowl.
Instead, they put it on its stand, and it gives light to everyone in
the house. In the same way, let your light shine before others, that
they may see your good deeds and glorify your Father in heaven
(Matthew 5:14–16).

Reflection
Light can't be seen, yet we cannot see without it. Light reveals
what would otherwise be veiled in darkness. In the light of day, we
can safely travel without tripping over obstacles or losing our way.
Evil often lurks in darkness, but light brings safety. Without light,
the world would be a frightening place: it would be unlivable
since, when there is no light, there can be no growth.

The star of Bethlehem reveals the Light of God has come
into the world; a light foretold by the prophet Isaiah.

The Servant of God in Isaiah 49 would be a lighthouse guiding all nations to salvation. Abraham was promised that his progeny would bless all peoples (see Genesis 12:3b). Throughout Israel's history, it waited for this Servant of God to appear and to fulfill God's promise. God promised to send his Servant to restore Israel's fortunes; that is part of Jesus' mission, but he was so much more than that—he was the one who would be the Light of the world.

In John's gospel, Jesus proclaims: "I am the light of the world" (John 8:12a). The Greek text of the gospel uses the grammatically unnecessary words, *Ego Eime*. Here, Jesus applies to himself the name that Yahweh gives to Moses before the burning bush: it is the name by which Moses is to identify God to the Hebrews when they ask Moses who sent him. *I am.*

Jesus is the world's light because the fullness of divinity resides in Him. God came into the world in a stable in Bethlehem; with that sacred birth, a light shone that can never be overcome by darkness. In His birth, life, ministry, teaching, and death, Jesus reveals the character of God: God is infinite self-gift; God is love.

As Jesus' disciples, as the people who have faith in Him and love Him, we are also to be the light of the world. Like Jesus, we are God's sons and daughters. John's gospel assures us that: "[T]o all who did receive him [Jesus], to those who believed in his name, he gave the right to become children of God" (John 1:12). Our lives lived in faith are an extension of Jesus' own life and ministry. We are extensions of His divine love and compassion.

We are to be other Christs until He comes again.

Prayer

Lord, You illumine our lives and our world. Your presence gives us clarity, safety, and peace. In troubled times, when so many voices call us to follow them, give us the wisdom to follow You alone. Your message of compassion and kindness guides us as we journey through life. You have sent us Your Spirit as our advocate and guide. You tell us that if we live our lives, we must lose them as we follow You on the Way of the Cross. Show us, each day, what our self-denial must mean for us to be Your disciples. Keep us faithful to You in our twisted, changing world until we finally come to the joy of Your Kingdom, where we will live with You in unity with the Father and Spirit forever. Amen.

Activity

In prayer, ask the Lord how He wants you to reflect His divine light. Perhaps He wants you to begin praying more with your spouse, your kids, your parents, or some neighbor. You could start by simply asking (without being pushy) someone close to you to join you in prayer. It doesn't have to be a long prayer—you could start simply with a prayer before or after a meal, or maybe prayers at bedtime. Perhaps you could ask a colleague at work to join you in grace before you share lunch. These are all simple ways to bring the light to others and to raise their consciousness of God's presence. You could invite a neighbor with no faith community to join you at church on Sunday, then go with them so they don't have to walk into church alone.

Write about how the Lord responds to your prayer, what you do next, and what comes of it in your prayer journal.

#

Notes

The Sixth Day of Christmas

Scripture

"When the time came for the purification rites required by the Law of Moses, Joseph and Mary took him to Jerusalem to present him to the Lord (as it is written in the Law of the Lord, 'Every firstborn male is to be consecrated to the Lord'), and to offer a sacrifice in keeping with what is said in the Law of the Lord: 'a pair of doves or two young pigeons'" (Luke 2:22–24).

Reflection

"Consecrate to me every firstborn male" (Exodus 13:2a). Joseph and Mary follow the law of Moses. As their firstborn son, the Torah required His parents to consecrate Jesus to the Lord as a sign and reminder that the mighty actions of the Lord rescued Israel from Egypt. Because childbirth also made a mother ritually unclean under Mosaic law, Mary also had to go through certain purification rites, including sacrificing a pair of turtledoves as a burnt offering and sin offering.

These two offerings symbolize the profound and weighty nature of a parent's love: aspirational and directional. Aspirationally, the offering represents parents' dreams for their child at the outset of his life. Directionally, it serves as a poignant reminder of the sacrifices parents must make as they guide their child's growth in wisdom, age, and grace before the Lord.1

From the very beginning, Jesus' presentation and Mary's purification remind us that the incarnation takes place within the sacred story of the Jewish people. Mary and Joseph were pious, practicing Jews, and they raised their son Jesus to know the God of Abraham, Isaac, and Joseph. Jesus would later teach that he had not come to abolish but to fulfill the law of Moses and the promises of the Prophets—a divine plan of continuity and completion.

As we again see toxic antisemitism raging throughout the world, Christians must remember that our Lord and Savior lived and died a Jew. While He criticized the corrupt Jewish elites all His life, He was faithful to the law of God, His Father. He lived and died to restore Israel, not to condemn it. His first followers, our forebearers in faith, were all Jews. As Christians today, we are all, in a way, Messianic Jews: Jesus calls us into the promises made to Abraham and asks us to share His love for His people. We cannot remain silent when powerful interests in the United States and around the world are again calling for the eradication of not only the Jewish state but also the Jewish people.

We must speak out against hatred of the Jews; we must act to support and defend our Jewish friends and neighbors both in our neighborhoods, in our nation, and around the world.

Your voice matters—use it!

Prayer
Creator God, You called Abraham and promised to make him a great nation through which all the earth's nations would be blessed. In Jesus, that promise was fulfilled. He was born of Mary, a young Jewish girl who loved and served You with purity and faith. From the beginning of His life, Jesus was taught to honor and keep Your law, which he came to fulfill. In compliance with Torah law, Jesus was consecrated to You. His consecration looks back to the time when You saved Your people from slavery in Egypt, and it looks forward to the cross when he saves all creation from sin and death. Thank you, Father, for the great people of Israel, for the promises You made to Abraham, for the challenging message of the prophets, and for Your never-failing love for Your people.

Please give us the courage to protect the people of Your promise by lifting our voices against all forms of hatred directed at the children of Abraham or for that matter, anyone. Amen.

Action

At this time particularly, when hatred of Jews has again become fashionable in certain circles and on college campuses, take a stand against antisemitic bigotry. Speak a word of encouragement to a Jewish neighbor who may feel frightened by the tenor of the hatred of Jews now prevalent throughout the world. Finally, pray for peace in the land the Lord made holy. Pray for the peace of Jerusalem. Pray for religious tolerance across the globe.

\#

Notes

The Seventh Day of Christmas - The Holy Family

Scripture

"When Joseph and Mary had done everything required by the Law of the Lord, they returned to Galilee to their own town of Nazareth. And the child grew and became strong; he was filled with wisdom, and the grace of God was on him" (Luke 2:39–40).

Reflection

They looked so normal: a Jewish couple and their firstborn son living a quiet, pious life in their home village. Joseph, his new bride, and their son looked like any other young family of the time and in that place. After the angel announced Jesus' birth and Mary's virgin pregnancy; after the shepherds worshiped and the angels sang; after the magi and their gifts came and went and the star left the sky; after a harrowing escape to Egypt and a safe return, they were finally home to live a quiet life of love, learning, and growth.

Having fulfilled the law's obligations, the holy family led a modest family life, demonstrating the sanctity of family. Joseph and Mary instilled in their child the faith of Israel. Like any other child, Jesus had to learn about the God who was His father. Yes, He was always divinity in human form, but he was also truly and completely human, like us in all but sin, so he needed to learn, and Joseph and Mary were his teachers.

Like every child, Jesus learned to speak, walk, and play with other children. As Jesus grew older, Joseph taught him carpentry. Jesus helped around the home with chores, and when His siblings were born, He helped care for them. He also learned the faith of

Israel. Mary and Joseph were devout Jews who taught Jesus about God's promises to Abraham. They taught him to know and observe the Mosaic law, God's gift to the Jews. He knew the Exodus story and reenacted it, as every Jewish family has done since the time of the Exodus. Jesus learned of Israel's sin and God's patient love and forbearance. He grew, Matthew tells us, not only in age but in wisdom. Jesus' early life, normal as it was, prepared Him for His saving mission.

The simple is sacred! Like Jesus' early years, our lives are mostly quiet and uneventful, but even in those times, God is present, molding and shaping us in preparation for the work He gives us to do. Nothing escapes the power and presence of God's Spirit. When we consider things unimportant or even trivial; God is present. As the patriarch Jacob realized after his dream at Bethel: "Surely the Lord is in this place, and I was not aware of it" (Genesis 28:16b).

Prayer
Dearest Lord, You have made the ordinary moments of our lives sacred because you are present there. Make our families sacred places where we can live in Your love and grow in Your grace. Spirit of wisdom, our advocate and friend, fill us with Your grace and let us see the face of Christ in all those around us, especially the old, the weak, the suffering, and the poor. Amen.

Activity
Meditate for twenty or more minutes about the presence of God in the simple things around us: nature, our loved ones, and the people God draws into our lives for purposes known only to Him. After your meditation, write about this in your prayer journal.

#

Notes

173

The Eighth Day of Christmas

Scripture

"So they [the shepherds] hurried off and found Mary and Joseph, and the baby, who was lying in the manger. When they had seen him, they spread the word concerning what had been told them about this child, and all who heard it were amazed at what the shepherds said to them. But Mary treasured up all these things and pondered them in her heart. The shepherds returned, glorifying and praising God for all the things they had heard and seen, which were just as they had been told.

On the eighth day, when it was time to circumcise the child, he was named Jesus, the name the angel had given him before he was conceived" (Luke 2:16–21).

Reflection

The incarnation was the most significant event in human history. God took on human flesh and became one of us. In doing so, God revealed the potential of our humanity: to hold divinity within it. The infant, lying in a cattle trough turned into a crib, embodies the ineffable mystery that lies at the heart of things. The creator of the universe is there, in a crib. Everything changes when Jesus is born. The very poverty of the setting reveals much about the character of the God of Abraham, Isaac, and Jacob: the God who reveals himself in history.

His ways are clearly not ours. By God's choice and the angel's announcement, this simple, poor, illiterate child (probably in her early teen years) is the mother of the long-awaited Messiah. She is the mother of God. Despite her humble state, all generations have indeed called her blessed. Jesus' mother, Mary, is now acknowledged as the mother of all Christians and the Church.

God truly does exalt the humble even as he humbles the exalted.

Then there are those shepherds! They have terrible jobs: no woman of the time prayed that their sons would grow up to be shepherds. Sheep are sweet but defenseless animals. Shepherds worked long hours and received little reward for their efforts. Yet the Scriptures tell us David, the shepherd boy, was called to be king of Israel, a man after God's own heart. The prophets frequently speak of God himself as the "shepherd of Israel," who would shepherd the people with love and care, binding up the wounded, tending to the weak, and bringing the lost back into the fold of God's people.

Shepherds may have been low on the social totem pole of ancient Israel, but their love and care for their sheep was legendary. God chose to reveal the greatest miracle of all time not to priests or potentates but to the humble and weak: simple shepherds tending their flocks at night.

God cares for those who live on the margins: the poor, the unsophisticated, the humble, and the weak. They are the ones who first hear the good news of Jesus' birth. They asked no questions and did not hesitate a bit. No, they rushed off to see with their own eyes the great things that God was accomplishing. When they found the miracle, it wouldn't have looked too miraculous to most observers, but they saw Mary, her husband Joseph, and the baby in His straw bed and knew the God of Israel was again entering the history of His people and the world.

Having seen the Child and His parents in that stable in Bethlehem, the shepherds returned home rejoicing and sharing the good news with others, who shared their amazement. The shepherds show us our role in God's plan: not to keep the miracles of faith in our hearts alone. God wants us to share the wonder of His love, manifest in the Christ Child and later on the cross, with others.

With those shepherds, let us glorify and praise God for all He does in our lives and world.

Prayer

Thank You, Father God. You are the Lord of heaven and Earth. All creation glorifies You. When Your Son, Jesus, was born, He humbly shed his divinity and took on our nature with all its frailty. His mother was a humble young girl. He was born in a stable, and His first crib was a cow trough. Shepherds were the only witnesses to the great miracle of His divine incarnation.

In Jesus' birth, You show us Your love for all Your children, especially the poor, weak, humble, and lowly. Open our eyes to see our own poverty as we come before You. We have nothing other than what You allow us; we are nothing other than what You allow us to be.

Help us see Your presence, power, and love in our own lives and the lives of all we meet. When we meet the least of our brethren, we meet You. When we see You, whether or not we recognize You in the moment, may we give You a drink if You thirst, food if You are hungry, and clothes if You are in need. We ask this in Jesus' Holy Name. Amen.

Actions

Our world is full of people in need. Do something to alleviate the suffering of some person in your community who is lonely, hungry, poor, or struggling. Do it because helping that person will give the Christ Child the kind of Christmas present he longs to receive.

Find some way to share God's wonderful work in your life with someone else. God is great, so be grateful. Keep a journal recording all the gifts God gives you, big and small. In that journal, record not only what God has done in your life, but also write a prayer of gratitude each day. Keeping this journal and writing those prayers will bring you great joy—I guarantee it!

#

Notes

179

The Ninth Day of Christmas

Scripture

"We know that we have come to know him if we keep his commands. Whoever says, 'I know him,' but does not do what he commands is a liar, and the truth is not in that person. But if anyone obeys his word, love for God is truly made complete in them. This is how we know we are in him: Whoever claims to live in him must live as Jesus did" (1 John 2:3–6).

Reflection

Jesus came to give us life, but not any old life. He came to give us eternal life. God became human to show us the potential of our own being; humanity was created to hold divinity. Jesus is the archetype—God created humanity to hold divine life perfectly, as it does in Jesus' human nature. Disciples learn from the teacher: to follow Jesus is to live as He taught us to live. No one does this perfectly, but we should strive each day to be more Christlike than the day before. The Reign of God is not something to wait for in heaven: it's here, it's now, it's around us, it's within us.

Our true connection with Him is established when we lead a life that mirrors the life Jesus would lead if He were living our lives. This is the ultimate purpose of life and every single day of life. It's the essence of the incarnation of the divine. We not only have the potential to become like Him, but we must strive towards this likeness daily.

We can only become like the Lord by adhering to His commandments. Unlike the Torah with its 613 commandments, Jesus simplifies the law without abolishing any part of it. When asked which of the 613 laws of the Torah was the greatest, Jesus combined two commandments that surpass all others.

The Torah instructs us to "Love the Lord your God with all your heart and with all your soul and with all your strength" (Deuteronomy 6:5). To this, Jesus adds that we must love the Lord with "all your mind" (Mark 12:30). Jesus also includes a second commandment found in Leviticus: you must "love your neighbor as yourself" (Leviticus 19:18; Mark12:31). The second great commandment is "like" the first: you can't have one without the other, they are two sides that conclude "There is no commandment greater than these" (Mark 12:31).

There is the challenge of living a Christ-like life in all its simplicity and difficulty. It boils down to love. Unfortunately, love has become an overused word. People say they love hats, celebrities they have never met, or a cold beer on a hot day. This is not the robust love Jesus is calling us to. "'As I have loved you,' he said, 'so you must love one another'" (John 13:34).

What is the love of Jesus like? It is generous and giving. On His cross, He pours out everything He had and everything He was, to the last drop of His blood, for us, His beloved, though unworthy brothers and sisters. Our love requires us to give as He did, even unto death.

Jesus' love was forgiving. His words on the cross are among the most important ever uttered by anyone: "Father, forgive them, for they do not know what they are doing" (Luke 23:34). If we are to be like Him, we must forgive, hold no grudges, and love with an abundance that touches even our enemies.

Finally, Jesus' love is unconditional, with no strings attached. So must ours be. In that way, we bring His light to the world around us.

Prayer

Faithful Lord, Your love knows no limits, and Your forgiveness touches and transforms the lives of sinners who hear your voice and accept your good news. The world only knows you through us, your disciples. Give us eyes that see with generosity and kindness. Give us hands like yours that touch lovingly and heal. Give us a voice that brings hope to the weary and lost. Let us be your agents in this twisted and broken world. Fill us with the Spirit so we might say, with Paul, "I no longer live, but Christ lives in me" (Gal. 2:20). Let me be a blessing to all whom I meet because in me they meet You, and in You alone can they find life. I ask this in Your Holy Name: You are One God with the Father and the Spirit. Amen.

Activity

How can you live a more Christlike life in your community, with the family God has given you, and in your workplace or school? Take thirty minutes and write a journal entry about this question. Then, decide what you will *do*. Remember, Christianity requires being doers of the Word. How will you love better, forgive more, and extend your generous love to others who desperately need to feel the healing presence of Christ through you?

\#

Notes

The Tenth Day of Christmas

Scripture

"See what great love the Father has lavished on us, that we should be called children of God! And that is what we are! The reason the world does not know us is that it did not know him. Dear friends, now we are children of God, and what we will be has not yet been made known. But we know that when Christ appears, we shall be like him, for we shall see him as he is. All who have this hope in him purify themselves, just as he is pure" (1 John 2:1–3).

Reflection

When I was studying theology, Andre, one of my fellow students, a guy from the Midwest who I thought to be a bit goofy, would habitually address friends and strangers alike as "child of God." I'd run into him in the cafeteria, and he would greet me in the most cheerful of tones: "Good morning, child of God!" I thought it (and him) to be a bit hokey and off-putting. The word *unctuous* comes to mind.

I was wrong!

Andre, I now realize, was a holy man who knew whereof he spoke. Greeting me and countless others as "child of God" was a powerful reminder of the most fundamental aspect of my life. It still is. Recalling those greetings now, years later, reaffirms the most important aspect of my identity. I have played many roles: a husband, father, grandfather, friend, neighbor, student, teacher, pastor, attorney, writer… the list can go on. But more important than any of those roles is the name God Himself has given me. I am His adopted son, His child. This realization has transformed my life and continues to inspire me.

Children are valued members of the family. In 1 John 3, John explains that when we are God's children, we can no longer live as children of the world. We are called to a higher standard to live lives that reflect our divine heritage. We can no longer live sinful and idolatrous lives, lusting after what the world tells us to seek: power, wealth, selfish pleasure. Instead, we must choose the love of others over ourselves, guided by the light of God's love.

The essence of idolatry is to put someone or something else ahead of God. America has its fair share of idols: politicians, entertainers, business moguls. None of these people are bad in themselves, but we have gone astray when we turn to them for salvation and follow them rather than God's righteousness. Ideologies can also take God's place. Marxism, for example, replaces God with the Marxist state. The twentieth century gives ample testimony of the lethal effect of allowing the government to play God.

As God's children, our high calling is to keep the God and Father of our Lord Christ Jesus on the throne of our hearts and reject all pretenders, no matter how powerful or persuasive. The powers of this world may put tremendous pressure on us to bend us to their will. Brutal persecutions often result when Christians resist the world's pressure to conform. Both national socialism in Germany during the Nazi era and international socialism, as we have seen in Communist China and Soviet Russia, persecuted and killed Christians who resisted the totalitarian demands of the Nazi or Communist Party.

Pressures to conform to the platform of the world and its rulers are now trying to force Christians to condone abortion on demand and the perversity of the LGBTQIA+ agenda. Our leaders expect us to turn a blind eye to homelessness, to the scourge of drugs flowing into our country over porous borders, confiscatory taxation, and a manifestly unfair justice system. Don't rock the boat or you will be cancelled.

What will we do about all this, child of God? Will we say nothing and do nothing? Will we hide from the reality that the liberty given us by our God is being eroded by corrupt and evil people?

We can and must do something.

God spoke to King Solomon at night after the dedication of the temple. The Lord knew His people would sin repeatedly and that He would need to punish them. He offers the king hope, though. He says: "If my people, who are called by my name, will humble themselves and pray and seek my face and turn from their wicked ways, then I will hear from heaven, and I will forgive their sin and will heal their land" (2 Chronicles 7:14).

In the face of a nation gone astray, the most important thing we can do is to seek God's face and turn away from evil in all its forms. Where do we find the face of God? A starting point is His Word, the Bible. We should all be reading it more to find inspiration for life. Through Scripture, we see it in the faces of the poor, the lonely, the sick, the old, the forgotten, and the forlorn.

Turning from our evil requires turning from our selfishness to again think of and help those who need our help the most. If we do that alone, the Lord tells us He will be moved to heal us as individuals and as a nation.

Finally, it's time to do as Jesus did throughout His life: fast and pray for a new, great awakening of faith throughout the world and the coming again of our Savior.

Prayer

Lord, come to Your people again. We have faith in You. Give us loving hearts so we might live as Your worthy brothers and sisters and as children of God, for that is what You gave us the right to be; that is who we are. In times of trial and tribulation, please help us to stand firm against the wickedness of this present age and the lies and snares of the Enemy. I want to live as the Father wills me to live in purity and righteousness. Help me in times of trial and temptation to remain faithful to my high calling as Your disciple and a child of God. I ask this in your Holy Name and through the Spirit, with the Father, You are One God forever. Amen.

Activity

Pray for a new great awakening of faith throughout the world. If your doctor permits it, fast for this intention as well. Then, seek the face of God in the suffering of your community. Do you have an elderly relative? Visit her. Where are there lonely people who might love to have a visit from you? Nursing homes are full of such folks; offer to volunteer in one of them, not just for a day but regularly. Write about experiences like this in your prayer journal. What do you experience when you find the face of God in the hungry, thirsty, poor, imprisoned, abandoned, or lonely? Remember, one day, we will hear the Lord remind us that whatever we did for the least of our brothers and sisters, we did for Him.

#

Notes

189

The Eleventh Day of Christmas

Scripture

"This is the confidence we have in approaching God: that if we ask anything according to his will, he hears us. And if we know that he hears us—whatever we ask—we know that we have what we asked of him" (1 John 5:14–15).

Reflection

Jesus lived, died, and rose so we, who believe in Him, might have life in all its fullness. This simple truth is at the heart of John's gospel. He tells us as much in the final word of chapter 20. The signs Jesus performed during His ministry, from changing water into wine at the wedding feast in Cana to raising Lazarus from the dead in Bethany, all contributed to answering the question: "Who is this man?"(Matt. 8:27).

John also answers that question by telling the story of Jesus' passion and death. Even in his passion, John shows us Jesus embracing the cross out of obedience to God's will. Jesus' faithfulness to our Father, even through His agony and death, reveals the glory of God as He rescues us from sin and death. The Father confirms Christ's glory in the resurrection.

Why did John tell the Jesus story? "[T]hese [signs] are written that you [the reader] may believe that Jesus is the Messiah, the Son of God, and that believing you may have life in his name" (John 20:31).

John writes his first letter to explain further what the life we have in Jesus means in concrete terms.

First, faith, as John understands it, is not merely the assent of the mind to some proposition or theory. Nor is it to learn and believe in Jesus' teachings. Faith is developing and deepening a vibrant relationship with the Lord through the Spirit. It is speaking with him regularly in prayer and striving to live as He would have us live. It is seeking to love as Jesus loved and who Jesus loved. This is how the world will recognize us as Jesus' disciples: by our love.

Second, when we have this kind of faith, we have eternal life. The eternal life of which John speaks does not give us immunity from physical death. Rather, John assures us that when our bodies die, we live on but differently. Our spirits continue to live with the Lord in the bliss of God's Kingdom. "I am the resurrection and the life," Jesus tells Martha at the tomb of Lazarus, "The one who believes in me will live, even though they die; and whoever lives by believing in me will never die" (John 11:25–26).

Finally, we can be confident in our prayer: God hears us as a loving father would hear a beloved child. Therefore, if we ask for anything good for us (anything following His will), we will be answered in ways better and more powerful than we could imagine. We may not immediately see the results, or, seeing them, we may not understand, but God, our Father, hears and acts on our behalf. All this is an aspect of being a child of God.

Prayer
Gracious Father. I come into Your presence knowing that You listen to me with love. Your Holy Spirit fills my heart and inspires my prayer. Increase my faith, deepen my prayer, and keep me walking every moment of my life in the sure knowledge that You are with me and will never leave me. Protect me from the tricks and lies of the enemy and give me the strength to resist

temptations. I ask this in Jesus' name and through the power of the Spirit. With You, they are One God. Amen.

Activity

Before you go to bed, take ten minutes to review your day. How much time did you devote to prayer, meditation, or reading the Bible? Our prayers matter. Pray for your loved ones, pray for sick family members or friends, pray for the world—it's quite a mess and needs God more than anything else. Pray for God's guidance in the decisions you make. And pray with gratitude for all that God has given you.

Prayers of gratitude are very important.

\#

The Twelfth Day of Christmas - the Epiphany

Scripture
"Arise, shine, for your light has come,
and the glory of the Lord rises upon you.
See, darkness covers the earth
and thick darkness is over the peoples,
but the Lord rises upon you
and his glory appears over you.
Nations will come to your light,
and kings to the brightness of your dawn" (Isaiah 60:1–3).

Reflection
Customarily, the twelfth day of Christmas is the feast of the Epiphany, when the church remembers the pilgrimage of the magi and the worship and gifts they brought to the child Jesus.

The Greek root of the word *epiphany* (*epi phanien*) means to shine over or to bring to light. The angels whom Luke tells us appeared to the shepherds on the hillside tending their flocks at night proclaimed the inbreaking of God's glory in the birth of the Child lying in a manger bed in Bethlehem. That Child would bring God's peace (*shalom*) to a world then, as now, mired in conflict and hatred.

Jesus' birth is the revelation of God's love and the fulfillment of God's promises to the Jews. The Child is the coming of the long-awaited Messiah. Something more is afoot, however. Jesus is significant to all the world, not just to His own people. The star of Bethlehem and the magi's arrival signal the universal significance of the nativity.

The star shines so *all* people can see it. The magi, gentiles coming from afar, follow the star to find a king worthy of their homage. Thus, the prophecy of Isaiah is fulfilled: the glory of the Lord has been revealed to the nations—all see it together.

The light that first shone over Bethlehem continues to shine today—in us! As Jesus' disciples, we are now the "light of the world." Our light shines when we engage the world as Jesus would engage it if he were living our life. It shines in our love and acts of kindness (even the little ones that often go unnoticed). It shines in our patience and forbearance. It shines in our forgiveness. It shines when we do what is right rather than what is easy or popular.

Living in loving obedience to God's will, we become examples of Christian love and virtue.

In the first centuries after Christ, the church grew exponentially in the Roman Empire, not because of the great preaching of the apostles and their successors nor because of the compelling writings of the church fathers (and mothers). It grew because, through two devastating plagues, Christians cared for one another and their neighbors. Unbelievers saw Christians lovingly caring for the sick and dying and they wanted to know about the Crucified God who inspired it.

"Let your light shine before others, that they may see your good deeds and glorify your Father in heaven" (Matthew 5:16).

Prayer

Lord, please fill us with Your light so we, too, can radiate Your loving presence in the world. Let our words and actions reflect Your presence and power. Through them, may we inspire people who do not know You to begin to seek Your face. Show us how to let our light shine each day so we give you glory and lead others to You.

Activity

The magi brought gifts to Jesus. What gift can you give him today? Write about this in your prayer journal. Then, get a surprise gift for someone you know who might need a little lift. Ask the Lord in prayer who you should bless this way. It doesn't have to be big or expensive. It does have to be given out of love. Now wrap it and have fun giving it, maybe with a greeting card.

#

Epilogue

Years ago, I heard a story that greatly impacted my life.

During World War II, bombing and artillery fire had reduced a church in Strasburg, Germany, to rubble. While the church was badly damaged, a statue of Jesus near the church's main altar was virtually unscathed, except that the hands of Christ, which had been outstretched, were missing. Someone had placed a crudely drawn sign at the statue's base that read, "I have no hands but yours."

Hundreds of years earlier, Teresa of Avila said as much and more. She wrote, "Christ has no body now but yours. No hands, no feet on earth but yours. You are the eyes through which he looks with compassion on this world. Yours are the feet with which he walks to do good. Yours are the hands through which he blesses all the world."

And so we are.

During the Advent season, we remember the anticipation with which the world waited for the birth of the Messiah. This season is a time of great anticipation and hope as we remember the fulfillment of the promise God made to Abraham to bless all nations with his progeny. He was the long-awaited Savior.

We also wait: the Lord who came once as a child in a manger will come again, in the fullness of time, to make His victory complete. We must be ready for Him when he comes again, Jesus pointedly and frequently reminded His disciples because while we do not know the exact day or hour, we know that the day will come, and the hour will be upon the world at some moment only known by the Father. At that time, we must be ready, like bridesmaids waiting to greet the bride and groom or like servants awaiting the return of their master.

Like the Jews in the time before the birth of Jesus, we are waiting for the return of the One who came and will come again. He tells us that when we see HIM next, He will come with judgment to make an accounting. How well did we invest the gifts (talents) with which we have been entrusted? When we saw the sick, the poor, the hungry, grieving, how did we treat them? Did we realize that when we were kind to them, we were being kind to the Lord? And if we ignored their plight, did we realize we had turned our backs on our Savior in disguise?

Advent and the Christmas season are times to reflect on the quality of our lives as we wait for Jesus' return. While we wait for the end time, what are we doing in the meantime? When God appeared in human form two thousand plus years ago, Jesus' people neither recognized nor accepted him. They were looking for something else: a person like David or Moses who would lead them with power out of the clutches of the Roman Empire to a restored kingdom of Israel. They were looking for what they wanted, not for what they needed. They wanted salvation from Rome's tyranny; Jesus came to free them from the grip of Satan and death.

Whatever the second coming will be like, you can be sure God will surprise us again.

While we wait, we must be ready to see the surprising Kingdom of God all around us. Remember, Jesus proclaimed that God's Kingdom is all around us, it is here, now, within us. Look at the events of each day with the eyes of faith. God appears in the small miracles we witness daily if we watch for them. He appears in the birth of a child, in the beauty of a starlit night, in the love of a friend, or in a life shared with a spouse. Jesus looks at us through the eyes of the poor, the lonely, and the frightened. Yet we will only understand this if we keep alert and watchful.

Prayer and reading Scripture will help us hone our watchfulness. So will regular meditation and worship in our faith communities. Unless we have a vibrant relationship with the Lord fostered by daily spiritual practices, we will have a hard time recognizing Him when He appears to us, or in the end when He comes again.

Our devotion to Jesus is more important than anything else we do. Ultimately, we will not care if we succeed, as the world judges success. The assets we accumulate will last far longer than we will. Soon, someone else will occupy that coveted corner office. The things we accumulate will deteriorate and decay. Only one thing matters: did we live the life God gave us as God willed us to live it? Did we find true joy, which can only be found by living a godly life?

When he comes again with the angels, will we be separated from the sheep or the goats? Will we hear Him utter these words to us: "Come, you who are blessed by my Father; take your inheritance, the kingdom prepared for you since the creation of the world" (Matthew 25:34)?

* * *